ABOUT THE AUTHORS

Valerie A. Reeves was educated at Newland High School, Hull and Hull College of Commerce. She has lived locally all her life and pursued various careers in Hull and Beverley. Currently she is working as a civil servant at Hull Prison. Her hobbies include painting, genealogy and animal charities.

Valerie Showan attended Kingston High School, Hull and Manchester University. She has spent her working life teaching English and Drama in schools in England and abroad. Her recent retirement from Winifred Holtby School, Hull has given her the leisure to enjoy her interests in travel, gardening and long distance walking.

D1313175

DAN BILLANY

Hull's lost hero

by
Valerie A. Reeves and Valerie Showan

Kingston **Press**

British Library Cataloguing in Publication Data.
A catalogue record for this book is available from the British Library.

First published 1999

© 1999 Valerie A. Reeves and Valerie Showan

Published by Kingston Press

ISBN 1 902039 01 7

Kingston Press is the publishing imprint of Kingston upon Hull City Libraries, Central Library, Albion Street, Kingston upon Hull, England HU1 2TF

Printed by Kingston upon Hull City Council Printing, 1-5 Witham, Kingston upon Hull, England HU9 1DA

Front cover: Dan Billany (1940). Photograph by Jerome of Hull.

To our other hero, Mr Rocket

ACKNOWLEDGEMENTS

Our especial thanks to Joan Brake, Dan's sister, for generously sharing her memories with us and allowing us access to Dan's unpublished works, family letters, photographs and other material. Without her help this book could not have been written. Our thanks also to Dan's cousins, Barbara Watson and Molly Todd, for memories of the Billany family and the loan of family papers. We are very grateful to Jim Tanfield, Dan's childhood companion, for his kindness and willingness to spend time talking with us.

We are indebted to Gaynor T. Johnson for her contribution of photographs and genealogical material and the support of Richard Kinns, John Markham and other members of the East Yorkshire Family History Society.

And thanks to all those who have helped us, including:
The staff of Hull University, particularly Sue Stephenson, Alumni Officer Mr & Mrs Reg Bloomfield, John Nicholson, Leslie Love, Leslie Brackstone, John Ketley and the staff from Chiltern Street School, J H Heald and Jean Barker from Hall Road School, Ken Worpole for his interest and advice, Major and Mrs Huddleston, Mary Mathieson, Herbert Thompson, Vic Wilson, Stephen Cloutier, Keith Killby of the Monte San Martino Trust, Roger Absalom, Elsie B. Read, Hull and East Riding Libraries, The Imperial War Museum, The Works Department, HMP Hull, Steve Howard of *Kingston Press* for his encouragement and faith in us

Extracts from *The Magic Door* by Dan Billany are reproduced by permission of Thomas Nelson & Sons Ltd. Extracts from *The Cage* by Dan Billany and David Dowie are reproduced by permission of Longman Group Ltd. Extracts from *The Trap* and *The Opera House Murders*, both by Dan Billany are reproduced by permission of Faber & Faber. T S Eliot's letter is reproduced by permission of Faber & Faber and the Eliot Estate. The extract from H E Bates' article is reproduced by permission of Laurance Pollinger Limited and the Estate of H E Bates. Thanks also to the Manchester Evening News and the Hull Daily Mail for permission to quote.

Photographs as indicated reproduced with permission from:
Mr & Mrs Reg Bloomfield, Barry Thompson, the Imperial War Museum.

PHOTOGRAPHS AND ILLUSTRATIONS

Preface

Who was Dan Billany? What does he mean to us? And why did we decide to write a biography of an almost totally forgotten writer? These are a few of the questions that ought to be answered before we begin our story.

It all started long ago, back in the late 1940s, in a Hull three-quarters destroyed by the war, a city of bomb-sites overgrown with rosebay willow herb and other weeds in their season. The number 15 bus took us to town each Saturday morning to change our books at Albion Street children's library and afterwards we would call in at Thornton-Varley's for a lemonade, sitting on tall stools in the upstairs cafe. We felt very grown-up at age nine, our library books in a shopping bag at our feet. They were the real object of the exercise for we were both avid readers anxious to share the exploits of Jennings, Biggles and The Famous Five. But we would try anything and did. Valerie's favourites were spine-chilling ghost stories, Val's horrifying adventures involving dungeons, rats, torture, the nastier the better. But we also loved comic stories, that's why Just William was such a hit with us. And then we discovered *The Magic Door*, subtitled *A Story for Boys*. We borrowed it week after week, we couldn't put it down, we acted out scenes from it and soon came to know great chunks of it off by heart, and we couldn't stop laughing at the jokes. If you read on you'll find out more about it and share some of the humour, but at this stage all we need to say is that it is the story of a school-teacher called Mr Rocket and his class of thirty boys, known as Standard Three. We hero-worshipped Mr Rocket. He was so funny, totally unlike any teacher we had ever met, more like a schoolboy himself and only just one step ahead of his high-spirited class.

And then of course we grew up and our pattern of life and choice of reading matter changed. Forty years later, on one of the rare occasions that we met, Valerie mentioned that she had discovered a second-hand copy of *The Magic Door*. Actually she said, "What does the name Mr Rocket mean to you?" Instant response and squeals of delight followed. Together we re-read the book. We even tried to interest our children in it but no joy. However to us it was as exciting, as fresh and as funny as ever. And to our surprise, we realised for the first time that it was all set in Hull, unnamed but unmistakable. So we investigated its author, whose name was Dan Billany; oddly enough we hadn't registered this as children. But it was difficult to discover any information about him beyond the fact that he had grown up in Hull and taught there for a while before joining the army in 1940.

We found three other books by him, all totally different, a detective thriller with as much blood and violence as anyone could wish, followed by two war stories, one concerning the war in the western desert, the other a personal account of two men interned in an Italian prisoner-of-war camp. An autobiographical note in the last of these hinted tantalisingly at an unsolved mystery as to the fate of the author. For the sake of Mr Rocket and those early years of devotion, we set about unravelling the story of Dan Billany.

It seemed he had been a writer of considerable note, his books high on best seller lists, translated into many languages, highly acclaimed in America, one a Readers Union Book Club choice, and all the subject of rave reviews at the time of publication. So why were all his books out of print, and even second-hand copies difficult to find? Perhaps it was the great divide of the Second World War that separated him from the following generation. He never did come home after the war, and it was not long before the tide of literature swept on with new preoccupations and Dan Billany was forgotten. It is very sad because all his books are eminently readable now and *The Magic Door* just as funny as ever.

It seemed wrong to us that such a talented writer should be forgotten in his home town. Hull has had many prominent and celebrated citizens over the centuries, but not so many that it can afford to neglect one of its outstanding sons. In his concern for the weaker members of society Dan Billany echoes Wilberforce, in his adventurous spirit Amy Johnson, and in his writing the genius of Andrew Marvell.

It was very difficult to find out anything about this man at all. The family had dispersed and for a while all we knew about his life was guess-work, reading between the lines of his novels. But eventually, by advertising in the local paper, we uncovered various leads and the ball started rolling to reveal a story worthy of any work of fiction. It begins in a poor dwelling in a terrace off Hessle Road and finishes in the winter snows high in the Apennine mountains. It involves not only Dan, but his remarkable family and their will to survive in the face of awesome odds. But most of all it is the story of an exceptional man, one of great intelligence, compassion, and determination, a man whom we came to know intimately as the story unfolded, and whom we hope you will enjoy meeting in the following pages.

Valerie A. Reeves and Valerie Showan
1999

CONTENTS

Chapter 1

Devon Street, Hull

"Oh for the wings, for the wings of a duck!
Far away, far away would I roam,
Oh for the wings, for the wings of a du-uck!"

Two small boys in short trousers and shabby boots, their arms about each other's shoulders, are swinging down the street, singing at the tops of their treble voices with tremendous emphasis on the word Duck. Suddenly they break apart.

"Have at thee for a scurvy knave!" yells Dan, the taller of the two, as he lunges forward with an imaginary weapon. Jim clutches his arms to his chest and with a horrible scream, crumples into the road, and lies there, kicking, a tortured gurgling coming from his throat. "Ha!" continues Dan, "'tis well for thee I left my trusty broadsword in the umbrella stand." Jim can't help but giggle in spite of the fact that he is now lying on his back twitching.

"Shut up you noisy buggers!" shouts Mrs Smith, from the doorway of number 66. "Can't you go and play somewhere else." At the same moment two figures are seen turning into the top of the street.

"Come on," says Dan, "let's go and chase Old Branson's chickens." And they dash off down the alleyway to the piece of waste ground behind the houses where, as well as the chickens, there's a pond and a wilderness of shrubs and long grass to play in.

Eva and Winnie approach down the street, tall and sophisticated for their nine years of age. With a pram to push (it contains Eva's little sister Joan, thankfully fast asleep) they feel very grown up, a world apart from their brothers' noisy, dirty games.

★★★

Devon Street was a quiet cul-de-sac of terraced houses, in a poor but respectable working class area, known as Dairycoates, which lay on the south side of Hessle Road. This is the main road leading west out of Hull, and as it plays a central role in the story, you should know that 'Hessle' is pronounced to rhyme with 'embezzle'. The Billanys lived near the bottom of

1

Devon Street, where it finished in a tiled alleyway abutting the back wall of Atkins Tin Works, which later became The Metal Box Company. The other end, nearest to Hessle Road was considered to be smarter; there the houses were larger with a front room, middle room, and back kitchen. Dan's best friend Jim Tanfield lived in one of these. Further down were the smaller houses and at the bottom was Hopkins' corner shop where the local housewives could pop in for odd items and a chat.

The Billany family, Mother and Dad, Eva, Dan and Joan, lived at number 73, a middle terrace house of yellow and red brick with two bedrooms with damp-stained ceilings over a front living room and a small kitchen. There was no bathroom, and no electricity; gas mantles lit the rooms with their gentle light. The kitchen was the heart of the home, with its black-leaded side oven, the kettle hanging on the reckon over the fire, the rubber rollered mangle, the gas oven and the white Belfast sink. In the cupboard under the stairs, which ran between the two rooms, was a bath with a wooden cover but, although it had an outlet pipe, there were no taps, no water - that had to be carried in buckets and poured in. The Billany children preferred the cosiness of the old tin bath in front of the kitchen fire. A visit to the lavatory meant going outside into the cold yard although some of the more enterprising tenants built wooden verandahs to roof over the coal house and outside WC.

Devon Street's surface was paved with stone flags and acted as the playground for the local youngsters. All the children joined in together; it was their social life, a hive of activity with nothing barred. In the warm summer evenings of the early 1920s the rhythmic swish and thud of the skipping rope turned by two willing fathers was heard amidst the chanting of skipping rhymes, the cries of kids playing 're-ally' or 'tag' or 'egg if you budge', and the clatter of jacks on the flags. Roller skates were all the craze then and it was quite possible to skate up Hessle Road as far as Pickering Park and hardly see a car. Dan did not skate; he tended to avoid sporting pursuits, but his sister Joan was an expert, able to do leaps, tricks and fancy steps; the skates appeared to be an extension of her feet and in her free time she rarely seemed to take them off. One day some strangers who had been watching Joan's agility on the roller skates approached her and offered to train her to perform in a circus. Joan was thrilled and dashed home to tell her mother who, of course, would not hear of her daughter being involved in such a thing. Joan was desperately disappointed but not surprised; Elsie Billany was very protective of her children - over-protective thought Joan. She tended to exaggerate any mishap into a disaster and a real problem took on massive proportions. One such was the day the oven blew up. Elsie scorned to use the old fashioned range built into the back kitchen. Instead she bought a small second-hand gas cooker. Unfortunately it hadn't been installed too carefully and there was a morning when Joan, playing in the street, was arrested by an enormous bang from the direction of her home. She dashed back to find the kitchen enveloped in smoke and her mother white and shaking in the yard; she had literally been blown out of her own back door. But there were no injuries on this occasion beyond scorched eyebrows and an apron in tatters.

It was relatively safe in the street, with the occasional horse and cart or bicycle passing by. The only car ever seen was that of the doctor and then only rarely. Trams were the usual method of transport then, not that they ran down Devon Street itself but clanged along the main road. After a long period of unemploy-

THE LORD MAYOR
(Councillor Mrs. Beattie Ware)

at first as a conductor, later as a dri-
t with his packed lunch, a tin of tea
er to him at the tram stop on Hessle

ng the residents of Devon Street and
Pa Crack were an eccentric old cou-
en's practical jokes, which included
in the front gate, imprisoning them
Winkles, aptly named as they ran a
or their jellied eels. There were the
was one very poor family, whose
it house, next to the alley, a sweet
on some glass and brought her in,
ng her home.
own up in the warren of streets and
sie fell for Harry the first time he
oung man too, with kind blue eyes
e. And what a talker! He knew so
had a lovely way of putting things
was a breath of fresh air, a straight-
he felt she could share her life.
n sisters who lived with their wid-
elped to look after the lodgers who
nily had for generations been asso-
ged fourteen, he was taken on as an
ilders. But he was impatient. He
ife's adventures so it was not long
rally ran away to sea. Several years
to strange ports in the far reaches

Elsie in 1910, he was twenty-three
d way of life. During the summer
rry was working on the docks at
aration. He longed for the week-
rry across the River Humber back

home to Hull. Elsie kept and treasured the postcards Harry sent her that autumn. Written in a beautiful copperplate hand, they vary from the frustrated

3

and depressed, to the excited and exuberant with touches of humour and high spirits thrown in. They are sometimes signed "Harry", but also "Cheeky Monkey" and his initials, HRB, rendered as "Aich Are Bee", this latter underlined with a row of linked Xs and the comment "You know what these are. Trellis work I don't think!"

As a result of his youthful impulsiveness, Harry found himself unqualified for anything except manual work. Occasionally he would sign on with one of the deep sea trawlers for a three week trip to Arctic waters. It was terribly hard work in appalling conditions but Harry was young and strong and saving up to get married. The crew were paid a share of the value of the catch and a successful trip could be very lucrative.

The couple were married at St. James's Church, Hull in May 1911. Elsie was twenty years old and very beautiful. She had a delicate featured face and luxuriant black hair which she wore looped back over her ears and drawn into a bun at the back of her neck. She was small and neat, elegantly dressed in a white silk blouse, frilled at the neck, with a dark skirt and jacket. They made a fine looking couple, Harry tall, smiling widely, confident about the future. Both were sensitive and intelligent young people, although they had had only the most basic of education; Elsie looked up to Harry as the one with the brains, but he was an idealist, an impractical dreamer, and in later years Elsie proved to be the one who held the family together with her good common sense and staying power.

They moved into a small house in Essex Street, the sort known locally as a sham-four, a cramped two-up-two-down, but they were delighted to have a home of their own. The front door opened into the living room, in the corner of which was the staircase; there was no electricity, nor hot water and of course the lavatory was outside. Harry, who was inventive and good with his hands, made basic pieces of furniture out of what wood he was able to scrounge, and with these and second-hand items given by family and friends, they set up house. Elsie, enjoying the role of proud housewife, made brightly coloured curtains and arranged flowers on the window-sills. But honeymoons don't last forever, and it was not long before Harry had to go back to sea leaving his young wife alone and pregnant. Her first child, Eva, was born in June 1912. It was a difficult birth, but Elsie's mother and sisters rallied round at the confinement and cared for the baby during the long period of recuperation. Harry continued his career at sea, now as an engineer in the Merchant Navy, signing on for long voyages with only brief periods of leave. The following year saw Elsie, pregnant again, having to cope alone but she resisted all attempts to give up her house and take refuge with her mother.

Her son Dan was born at 51 Essex Street on 14th November 1913. She named him after her dead father, Daniel Edward Wilson, but he was registered simply as Dan, with no middle name. Once again, Elsie took a long time to recover and was so weak that she was forced to move back to Carlton Street to live with her mother, who proved invaluable in looking after her and the two babies. When Dan was six months old, Harry came home and established his family in another rented sham-four at 73 Devon Street. This was to be the family's home for the next seventeen years. It had no better facilities than their previous home, but this house and the warm, supportive community of Devon Street were to be an important influence on all their lives.

★★★

Neighbours in Devon Street were neighbourly; this meant leaving doors unlocked, and helping out, when help was needed. Among the children there was little in the way of visiting, although their mothers would meet in each other's kitchens to gossip over a cup of tea. For the kids everything happened in the street. They identified strongly with their own territory; Devon Street maintained a rivalry with its neighbours Dorset Street and Essex Street, which at times developed into open warfare. Dan describes such a battle in *The Trap*, although this one is a nine year old's fantasy centring on a little girl in blue from the next street with whom he is in love.

> ... great hand to hand fighting would occur, broomhandles, half bricks and wooden swords figuring. Finally my men would break and fly, and I, fighting desperately, but gashed across the forehead with a brick, would be made prisoner by the soldiers of the girl in blue. They, and she, would torture me, and I would faint: and, as I lay semi-conscious, she would bend over and stroke my forehead, and her lips would be near mine - after this my fantasy became vague ...

Perhaps this was influenced by the young Dan's frequent visits to the pictures. The Eureka was the local cinema at the top of Devon Street on Hessle Road, an imposing name for an imposing building. Its white marble front was decorated with pediments and curlicues and the whole facade looked rather like a miniature Greek temple. But the children of the area didn't notice the architecture, nor did they have any idea that its name was Greek or what it meant. To them it was just the picture-house. These were the days before the talkies; the only noise came from the audience and the pianist employed to mirror the action in sound. One of Jim Tanfield's early visits there was with his sister Winnie when they were only about eight and nine years old. They were not normally allowed to go to the cinema in the evening but they had been so taken with the poster outside the Eureka for a film called *The Covered Wagon* that they begged their mother to be allowed to go. "Well," she said, "so long as you go with somebody else." They knew Dan and Eva would be going, they were regulars, so it was all arranged for Friday night - with the added incentive that there was no school next day. Dan explained that the best seats, the back half of the downstairs, cost eight pence, but children could get in for half price. So their mother gave them

5

four pence each and off they went. The story continues in Jim's own words.

"Well, we got to the cash desk and the girl looked down at us and said very sharply, 'No half price Fridays!' We were stumped. It was probably because this film was such an attraction. I think that Dan and Eva were the same as us with only four pence each. So Dan said, 'Well, we'll just have to go in the fourpenny seats.' 'OK,' we said. We didn't know any different. I can see us now following this torch, the four of us. The film had already started, it was well into the first showing. We followed the usherette's torch down the cinema, down and down and the screen got nearer and nearer and when we were right down at the bottom, we noticed that they had put forms in front of the first row of seats. Every seat was taken you see, even these forms were full because this film was such a big attraction. But we squeezed, the four of us, close together on one of these forms and looked up to watch the film. We were jolly nearly behind the screen looking up like this and all the figures were long and thin and the faces distorted. Anyway we watched it through. It was not long to the end as this was the first house, and then the moment the lights went up for the interval, Dan and Eva together whispered, 'Come on, quick!' We said, 'Where are we going?' But they had gone, straight to the back row of the fourpennies - they were veterans you see - and bagged the seats as people were leaving. We sat there for the whole of the second showing. And what a film. I've never forgotten *The Covered Wagon.*"

What happy, carefree days those were for youngsters growing up in the 1920s.

Chapter 2

Harry and Elsie Billany

The Hessle Road area of Hull was well-known for being a tightly-knit, independent community, particularly the district around the fish dock. People from other parts of the city used to look down on the Hessle Roaders as vulgar and threatening - the women (the fish-wives) had loud, coarse voices and the men were famous for their drinking. But it was nevertheless a very successful, close entity, fiercely protecting and supporting its own people. St. Andrew's Dock was at its centre. Here the fishing boats berthed and the many families whose livelihoods lay in deep-sea trawling lived in the packed streets and terraces nearby. Their common bond, the sea, held them together in a sort of brotherhood, or rather, sisterhood, for this society was of necessity matriarchal. The men were away for three weeks at a stretch, followed by a few days at home to discharge the catch and their wages, so running the family naturally fell to the women. Devon Street lay on the periphery of the trawling families' territory, but the inhabitants still felt they belonged to Hessle Road. Sadly, with the collapse of the fishing industry and wholesale slum clearance of the area, there now remains little sign of this once vibrant community.

Over many of the families in the area and especially the Billanys, there hung two serious interlinked threats: unemployment and ill-health. No work meant no money. Grim living conditions and no regular or reliable income were a recipe for weakness and illness and the poor, of course, were the very ones who could not afford to pay for medical treatment. The more provident families paid into a sick club and some doctors were willing to wait or even take payment in kind, but the worry was still there, a threat hovering in the background.

Dan's birth had been followed a year later by that of a sister, Peggy, in October 1914. She was a weak, ailing baby who died after a brief struggle lasting ten days. Harry loved his babies; he called them his 'chubbs', but in the early days he was not at home often enough to see much of them. With the outbreak of the First World War he joined the Royal Navy and was away from home for increasingly long periods, so his wife was left alone to cope with ill health, severe money problems and small children. Peggy's birth and death had been an agonising time for Elsie, but her spirits were revived by the birth of another daughter in 1916. This was Kathleen, a beautiful baby, who developed into a clever, delightful little girl. Harry did not see her until she was a year old, and he had to go back to join his ship soon afterwards. He was away from home too when in March 1919, she contracted diphtheria and died. She was two and a half years old. Elsie never got over Kathleen's death; there were more children, and more deaths, but Kathleen was the one who was ever present in her mind, the one she talked about, told her other children about and regretted for the rest of her life. From this time she was a changed person, and it was the turning point in her relationship with her husband. She could never forgive him for being away during the time of Kathleen's illness, and in her heart, she blamed him for her death.

Harry and his younger brother Mick had been keen to fight for their country once war with Germany had been declared. In 1914, Mick, twenty-three years old, joined the Flying Corps and served in France and later in Egypt, where he distinguished himself by inventing a furnace made out of metal cans for the disposal of waste. At its demonstration in the desert, the chimney caught fire and exploded with great effect, pieces of metal being strewn over a very wide area. In spite of this set-back, Mick rose to the rank of sergeant by the end of the war. Mick's real name was Neiles Boynton Billany but this was rarely used except by his mother. Sometimes the family affectionately referred to him as NBB2, to distinguish him from the grandfather after whom he was named and who was known as NBB1. But more about him later.

Harry, with his seafaring background, volunteered for the Royal Navy. In November 1915 he signed on as 7th engineer on HMS Hunstrick and for the next eighteen months he travelled the world on her. His job as an engineer kept him in the bowels of the ship, in cramped and sweltering conditions. If she had taken a direct hit he would have stood no chance of rescue and drowned or burnt, whichever came first. On one of his rare appearances on deck, he spotted what he took to be the periscope of a submarine in the vicinity. Petrified, he braced himself for the impact of a torpedo, but either it missed or he had been mistaken! Like his brother, he too was an inventor, and after the war he produced plans for a submarine escape hatch, all drawn out in meticulous detail, which he sent to the Admiralty; much later the plans were returned with a rejection note, but when a similar escape hatch made its appearance on Royal Naval submarines, Harry was convinced they had stolen his idea.

Both men returned unscathed at the end of the war only to face the prospect of unemployment in a country already sinking into the Depression. Mick was lucky and able to walk back into his pre-war job as a clerk at Priestman's, a prosperous engineering works in Hull. On Christmas Day, 1918, proudly wearing his sergeant's uniform, he married Olivet Fox. The family joked that they ruined everybody's Christmas, but actually, it was a great celebration, with the euphoria of the recent armistice adding to the young couple's hopes for the future. The bride came from a big family; she was one of nine children, and her father was a successful trawler skipper. Being fairly well off, they considered themselves a cut above the usual Hessle Road trawling fraternity and lived in some style in Edinburgh Street. It was here that Mick and Olivet made their home and lived comfortably with their in-laws for the first eighteen months of their marriage. Barbara, the first of their three children was born here, and when she was six months old, the family moved into a new council house on the recently completed Gipsyville Estate, north of Hessle Road. They felt they were really going up in the world - indoor plumbing and electricity!

For Harry, things did not go so well. Whilst Mick was looking forward to a successful career and prosperous family life, it was quite the opposite for his elder brother. It seemed that Mick had all the good luck and Harry had to make do with what was left. Shore based jobs were almost impossible to find, so he continued at sea until March 1919, when news of Kathleen's death and worries about his young family brought him home. But there was no work for him and consequently no money coming in. Worse still, his wife, in low spirits and poor health, was dismayed to find herself pregnant yet again, and now that Harry was unemployed, the situation seemed dire. Harry did his best to find work, travelling miles on foot even as far as the West Riding, picking up odd jobs here and there, but nothing sustained or secure. He considered himself lucky if he could send enough money home to cover the rent. Elsie had a terrible struggle to make ends meet, and as always in such situations, it was she who went without in order to give what she could to the children. She had a difficult pregnancy but was helped by the support of her mother, who cooked, cleaned and looked after Eva and Dan. They were seven and six years old when their sister Joan was born on 3rd December 1919.

After the birth, Elsie was very weak and took a long time to recover, but her mother came every day, often bringing a few provisions, such as potatoes, eggs, or butter. Once they had eaten and cleared away the tea table, Harry would take down his one-stringed fiddle, a relic of his sea-faring life, and play them keening, melancholy tunes as they sat in the firelight, with a glass of beer to hand. Years later, Dan wrote about this period of his family's life. He said of his Grandma Wilson "She was an angel to us." And this is how he described her. "She wore a little black coat which she seemed to have had all her life, and a black hat with a spray of cherries in the band - she pinned it to her thick white hair with a dangerous hatpin. Happy those early days, no matter that food and money and coal were scarce."

Slowly things improved. Harry was able to pick up more and more odd jobs so that there was money to pay the rent. For a brief period he and a friend set up a carpentry workshop, but there wasn't enough demand to make it viable.

Once she had regained her strength, Elsie embarked on a small business venture of her own, selling clothes to the factory girls from Atkins Tin Works who passed by number 73 on their way to work. Elsie bought her stock from Myers warehouse in Osborne Street. She should not have been permitted to buy wholesale as she had no shop premises, but the manager, who had taken a shine to her, allowed her to trade at his store. She sold garments such as underwear, dresses, stockings on the club system, her customers paying off their debts in small weekly amounts. If they did not call in with their payments, she had to collect the money, which often meant visiting homes in the rougher districts like Madeley

Street and Wassand Street. Dan sometimes accompanied his mother and on one occasion entered a room where a hugely fat woman was propped up in bed, probably permanently. The woman yelled, "Coom ovver 'ere and be bashed!" to a small boy in the room with her - and he did! Dan related the story with great glee at tea-time. Elsie's little venture ended when the owners of a drapery shop on Hessle Road made a complaint to her wholesalers. They lived in Devon Street and were likely to be very aware of her activities. So the business, which had been running maybe three or four years had to close.

Despite the lack of money, in these early days Christmas customs were celebrated in style by the Billany family. Out came the best cutlery, glassware and pottery proudly set out on a new tablecloth; nuts and tangerines appeared, even a bottle of rum. Dan captures the atmosphere in *The Trap*. One is reminded of the Cratchits' Christmas dinner.

> ... other delicious smells came in from the kitchen - the sharp sweetness of apple-sauce, the mouth-watering smell of roast chicken, the warm tang of rum, and a deep, rich, dark, fruity incense which could only be Christmas pudding. Then Mam carried in the chicken smoking hot, tiny sizzling crepitations popping all over its brown crisp skin, its chopped legs pointing at the ceiling, and Dad took up the carving knife and fork which had, apparently, been hidden for six months in the tin chest: the meal was on!

There would be few presents, each child receiving a stocking with sweets, a book or toy and some coins. Until the better years when they could afford a Christmas tree, Harry used to make a 'mistletoe', a zeppelin-shaped structure made from bent lathes fastened together and designed to dangle from the ceiling. Once the wood was covered in paper and the whole thing hung with toys and baubles, the effect was magical, so attractive in fact, that one year, to the family's consternation, Dan gave away the whole thing, toys and all, to a visitor who admired it.

★★★

Eventually, Harry found regular work as a carpenter and joiner and there was an income of about two pounds ten shillings a week coming in. They acquired a piano, at which Elsie was an accomplished performer, and the family would enjoy musical evenings singing together, the one-stringed fiddle wailing in the background. There was also a wind-up gramophone and a growing collection of records. Joan, now a toddler and a born performer, loved to dance and strut to the banjo solo in *Darkies' Holiday*, often wearing a black curly wig from an old concert party outfit of her father's. Things seemed to be looking up.

But Harry had ignored the doctor's warnings that Elsie's health would be seriously threatened if she were to become pregnant again. In April 1921, another baby, her sixth, was born. It was a boy and she named him Harry, but he was a tiny, weak baby who survived only a matter of days. Later that year, disaster struck the family again in the cruellest of ways. Harry found that his persistent cough would not go away. He could not sleep; he would wake in the night in a hot sweat, and as the cough got worse, so blood began to appear on his handkerchief. He soldiered on for a while but eventually had to consult a doctor and his worst fears were confirmed. Tuberculosis was diagnosed and a fortnight later, in January 1922, he entered the sanatorium at Cottingham. He put a brave face on it, but deep down he was in despair. The doctor told him that there was every chance of a full recovery if he stayed there for six months. But how could he afford it? Apart from medical bills, he had rent to pay, children to feed and clothe, and no wage coming in. Worse still, Elsie had just told him she was pregnant again. Nevertheless, he stayed in the hospital, and Elsie had to suffer the humiliation of queueing two mornings a week to beg for help from the Relieving Officer, the only chance the very poor had of getting a few pence to keep the children from starvation. It must have been dreadful for Harry to see on visiting days that his pregnant wife was herself starving.

After four months, Harry discharged himself from the sanatorium, more or less cured, but he was left with a heart condition which was to stay with him for the rest of his life. And the experience had left Elsie very low. Her health had suffered badly during this time of deprivation and once her baby was born, she had to go into hospital for a series of operations which culminated in her being told she was unable to have more children. (That at least must have been a relief for both of them.) On her return home, although she was told to rest, someone had to look after the home and the family, so she just carried on. There was something wrong with the new baby, Pamela, too; the doctor said she would never walk or talk or grow to maturity, so amongst Elsie's other trials she had to tend an ailing baby who was not expected to live. However, Harry's health was improving steadily. For a while, he slept in a wooden hut, which Mick had helped him to build in the back garden; fresh air was the accepted cure for TB. It seemed to work, and eventually, in June 1923, he was pronounced fit, and taken on by Hull Corporation as a tram conductor. This was the turning point in his fortunes, but he was a changed man. Just as the death of Kathleen had broken Elsie's spirit, this illness diminished Harry; he was never the same again.

Pamela died one afternoon in February 1925 shortly after her first birthday. Joan, who had only just started school, came home at tea-time to see the baby lying on the settee with pennies on her eyes. Her mother explained what had happened with sadness and resignation, but she shed no tears.

Fourteen years after that hopeful wedding day, we find Harry and Elsie both crushed by ill health and battered by the problems of bringing up a family on the poverty line. Their relationship never recovered from the series of misfortunes, and although they continued to live together, they had little interest in each other's company. Both of them centred their existence on their three surviving children, Eva, Dan and Joan, ambitious for them all and living through their trials and successes. Elsie especially was a tower of strength, not only keeping house and looking after their material needs, but also directing and encouraging them in the areas she valued - education, honesty, family loyalty and above all, ambition to make something of their lives. She was an intelligent, refined person, with an attractive musical speaking voice, a cut above the general run of her Devon Street neighbours. But her sufferings of the past decade had hardened her, she seemed to live in a shell, strict in her standards and beset with sanctions against anything she felt might harm her family. Pocket knives were forbidden, the children were not allowed to play out after dark, in fact she was uneasy whenever they were out of her sight. She had a phobia about candles. "Dirty, messy things, they are," she would say, but what she meant was that she was afraid the children would burn themselves to death.

Although she loved them fiercely, she found it difficult to show her children the affection they needed, however much they strove to get close to her. Picture the scene on a winter's afternoon, Elsie relaxing in an armchair in front of the grate, and her little girl Joan, aged three or four, sitting on the floor at her feet sucking her mother's fingers, enjoying the taste of lemon juice, which Elsie rubbed on her hands to whiten them.

Joan found it easier to be close to her father and as a small child he would call her his "right hand man" when she helped him with his carpentry. He was a skilled cabinet maker, and she loved to pass him the tools and watch his deft touch as he caressed a fine piece of wood. Sometimes he would take the children out with him visiting old seafaring friends. The first time he promised to take Joan to visit Old Harbour, she thought they were going to see an old man. In fact they sat in the engine room of one of the ships tied up there and ate ships' biscuits, which she found most unpalatable.

In spite of all the trials of the early part of the marriage, they were a happy family, probably because both parents were united in a love for their children and determination to give them the best they could. It was a household where there was a great deal of communication, lots of laughter, music and interesting conversation, and Harry was at the centre of this. He was the smiling, jokey one, who spoke with passion about his pet subjects, like Socialism and the struggle of the Working Class; but it would seem that Elsie was the more intelligent one, thoughtful, perceptive and capable. Dan inherited the best qualities from both of his parents; this and the upbringing they gave him were to produce a very remarkable man.

Chapter 3

Boyhood adventures

In later years, Dan Billany often said what very clear memories he had of his childhood. He used these in his writing on many occasions and especially in *Paul*. This unpublished work is a series of essays, subtitled, *"Aspects of the struggle between children and grown-ups."* Paul is a student teacher and he contrasts his experiences in the classroom with episodes from his own childhood. It is strongly autobiographical, featuring both Dan's own teaching practice, and formative memories from his early years. Here he describes the agony of the eight year old asthmatic.

To lie awake night after night, sweating with the labour of breathing, tortured by suffocating asthma, is a hard sentence on a child of eight. At least, a man knows his enemy, but a child draws shocking correlations between the things which hurt him, so that each one of them bears with it some of the terror of the others. And Paul dare not move his hands even to straighten his pillow, since every movement cost him breath, and he feared deeply those periods, lasting five minutes or more, when he laboured to recover the oxygen wasted in an ill-considered movement. He dared not even shout to his mother to turn out the gas, though the cold, slowly wavering spiky blue flame had hypnotised him into dull terror. And if those who have never experienced the peculiar suffering caused by asthma would like to form some idea of its nature, let them try for a few minutes to breathe only a tenth as deeply as they normally do; and then let them imagine this lasting, not for a few minutes, but a week. But even so, to regain the child's world of eerie, uncomprehended frightfulness is impossible for the adult.

This was certainly written from experience. As a child Dan suffered from frequent bouts of asthma which completely incapacitated him and meant he had to miss weeks of school. At such times, his lively high spirits gave way to all manner of fears as he lay awake struggling to breathe. The Scott's Emulsion Man was a recurring nightmare. This figure, depicted on the label of the popular cod liver oil tonic, was a tall, gaunt man, dressed in black oilskins and sou'wester, who carried a dead codfish as tall as himself over his shoulder.

The Scotts Emulsion man came, in his oilskins, dripping with dank weedy ocean. On his back was the great fish, its gaping mouth at his ear, as if they kept up an interchange of inhuman secrets, and its wide eyes staring. This was the dreadful figure which pursued a leaden footed Paul along the nightmare passages of sleep. Darkness and loneliness everywhere, and silence ... Then the stairs would creak under a heavy weight.

13

Paul's heart-beats almost choked him; his agonised eyes were rivetted on the door. It opened very slowly indeed, as if the person outside took a humorous delight in the situation; and the Scotts Emulsion man, so tall that he came under the doorway in a stooping position, entered, his cold eye fixed on the helpless boy, the fish mouth at his shoulder. Scream! Scream? You can only lie paralysed and sickened with dread, while the Scotts Emulsion Man comes towards you.

When he was eleven years old, Dan was admitted to the same tuberculosis hospital where his father had been a patient three years before. The other children in the street watched in awe as the blue-windowed ambulance drove away, with Dan's white face and waving hand visible through the back window. He was taken to Cottingham Sanatorium, set in a quiet village, some miles north of the city and on higher ground where the air was clear and considered beneficial to those with respiratory problems. He spent several lonely weeks there, certainly he was in Ward 4 at Christmas 1924. The difficulties of travel from Devon Street to Cottingham and the strict rules over visiting hours must have made the short time spent with his mother and sisters very precious to him. Although he did not have TB, it was thought that a period of rest and fresh country air would help him overcome his asthma and bronchitis. And the treatment worked, although he was not entirely free of the condition until adulthood.

As the young Dan grew stronger, his horizons expanded beyond Devon Street and the area outside his house door. He moved about with a small gang of lads, looking for fun, mischief and adventure. It was easy to find fun at the annual Hull Fair, held in October. This event was, and still is, the largest travelling fair in England and one of high spots of the year for Hull youngsters. Dan and Jim Tanfield were among its strongest supporters. The site is now tarmacked but at that time it was just a muddy field. The authorities tried to dry up this mess by spreading black sand from the foundry of the National Radiator Company. The result was oozing black mud, deadly underfoot.

Nowadays the rides and roundabouts whizz their riders past in a dazzle of flashing lights and howling pop music; in the twenties and thirties things were slower and gentler. Music was provided by the Gavioli type organ or barrel-organ and the roundabouts, although exciting enough for their patrons, might appear tame stuff to us: the galloping horses, stately and elegant, the ghost train and cake-walk, the 'Windy-hole', always well attended by groups of youths hopeful of seeing the girls' skirts blown up, and the 'Table-top', tilting and sliding its passengers. For the really daring spirits, the 'Shamrock' steam driven yacht was the ultimate in thrills, a giant swinging boat enclosed by rope mesh through which the riders looped their arms and braced themselves to be tipped slowly forwards and backwards, further and further, until the boat hung vertically before it swung back again. Dan persuaded Jim to venture on the Shamrock only once; after the ride Jim turned green and was sick behind the galloping horses but Dan just laughed with exhilaration and went back for more.

Nearer to home there were more everyday adventures to be had. In the early 1920s, a new estate of council houses was being built at Gipsyville, the other side of Hessle Road, within easy reach for gangs of boys looking for mischief. The half-built houses, encircled by scaffolding and supporting ladders were an ideal playground. Dan describes the scene in *Paul*.

Six or more corporation houses to a block, and any number of blocks, with here and there between them a cement roadway appearing, constructed in section, with long iron reinforcing rods sticking out and lying about. Straw was blown all over from where the men had been unpacking baths and drain pipes; snow-white lime of a creamy consistency, but coated at the top with grey, lay smoothly in square enclosures made of planks. Into this beautiful creamy stuff the boys threw stones, and prodded it with sticks. It fascinated them more than plasticine. Large heaps of cement and mortar, with spades sticking in them. Heaps of gravel, heaps of pebbles, heaps of granite chips, heaps of sand. Rubber water-pipes bound with wire, fastened to taps which could only be turned on with a key, Cementy buckets. Three stages of scaffolding, but the top stage incomplete and risky. The middle stage, below the bedroom windows clearly the best. Twelve feet from the ground, and accessible by many ladders. But the important thing was the multiplicity of possibilities provided by the three stages.

The boy Paul is collared by a bobby, who catches him larking on the scaffolding and gives him a severe talking to. Whilst listening to the policeman, Paul weighs up his chances of getting away with only a warning by a show of extreme politeness and contrition. It worked. And the policeman did not fulfil his threat to tell his father. Dan or one of his friends may well have had similar good luck.

For the whole period that they lived in Devon Street, the two older Billanys were friends with the Tanfields. Eva and Winnie were inseparable as children, so it was natural that Dan should pal up with Winnie's younger brother, Jim. For many years, they shared adventures and close shaves. Dan, a year older, was the leader and Jim was content that this should be so. Dan taught him to ride a bike - "Just grab the handlebars and push it away from you – See!" Years later, he took him on some hair-raising motor-bike rides.

Dan was fun to be with; he was full of ideas about places to go, he devised exciting variations on games, and was always ready with jokey patter, such as, 'A descent from the sublime to the gastric!', which followed his rendition of 'Oh for the Wings of a Duck'. He invented skits on all manner of songs and would recreate the most gripping scenes from the latest film at the Eureka. As they grew older, Jim realised that Dan was far and away more intellectual than he was, but the knowledge never affected their friendship. Even as a boy he was aware that Dan was different, and would make his mark in the world, hadn't Mr Dunham, his teacher at Selby Street West School said so?

Chapter 4

Who were the Billanys?

Just inside the gates of Hull's West Park, there used to stand an elegant drinking fountain. A marble bowl with four metal cups, hanging on chains, was surmounted by an ornate canopy, decorated in fine detail, its domed roof held up by four slim pillars. The inscription read:

Erected in memory of
Neiles Boynton Billany 1826 - 1896
Freeman of the city of Kingston upon Hull
and Tireless Worker against Injustice.

The Billany children were proud to see the family name carved on a monument and would often make a detour on the way home from school to admire it and to show it off to their friends.

— Who was he anyway?
— He's our ancestor and he was a famous citizen of Hull. Look, it says so there.
— And what sort of a name is that when it's at home? Whoever heard of anyone called Neiles Boynton?
— It's pronounced "Nee - lus" and it's a real name. My uncle is called it too.
— Nah he's not! Everyone knows your uncle. He's called Mick.
— Well, who was this "Nee - lus", and what did he do?
— Oh, I dunno ... Come on, race you to the swings.

★★★

The family story starts well over 200 years ago, in the 1750s, when Jonas Nilsson Gravelius was born in Sweden. His ancestors were firmly rooted in the little town of Anundsjö which lies near Sweden's eastern seaboard and where his grandfather was the assistant vicar and schoolmaster. But Jonas followed his father Nils' trade and went to sea. His early years are a mystery but in 1794 he turned up in London. By this time he had acquired a wife called Martha, a son Thomas and a daughter Sarah. A document dated this year still survives amongst the Billany family papers which describes Jonas as being forty-four years of age, five foot three and a half inches tall, with a "brown" complexion, no doubt weatherbeaten, as would be usual in a seafarer, and "wearing his own greyish hair" - presumably as opposed to a wig. The paper also stated that he was a foreigner and a subject of the King of Sweden. It was vital for Jonas to carry this on his person at all times to thwart the attentions of the press gangs which were then dangerously active.

At the end of the eighteenth century, Hull was the centre of the flourishing whaling trade and Jonas, an experienced seaman, moved to the town to seek his fortune. The whaling grounds were in dangerous waters, the Arctic Sea and the Davis Straits. All sea-going at this time was a hazardous business but whaling particularly so; the seamen had not only the weather and the sea itself to battle against but a powerful monster capable of crushing the fragile boats and drowning all their crew. It was a very risky occupation, but one of tremendous excitement. And the rewards were great, especially if one was an owner or part-owner, as so many products were obtained from the whale and the trade supported a host of subsidiary industries in Hull. The whaling trade reached its height in the 1830s, after which it gradually declined.

Jonas Gravelius died in April 1816. Surprisingly, his death is recorded in Sweden, near to where he was born. Was he at home on a visit? Had he perhaps separated from Martha and the children? We may never know but Martha was left in Hull, a widow, with Thomas and Sarah who were by now adult. Less than a year after her father's death, Sarah married at Holy Trinity Church in Hull. Her husband was George Billany, a mariner, also of Hull. The couple do not appear to have had any surviving children for several years until Neiles Boynton Billany was born on 25th April 1826, followed three years later by a brother, George.

The boys were only young, Neiles five and George two, when their father's ship was wrecked off Nova Scotia in 1831. Five survivors struggled to land, then decided to split into two groups to search for help. The group of three made it to safety but the others, George Billany and his companion, disappeared and were never seen again.

So at forty-four years of age, Sarah was left a widow with two young sons to bring up. Fortunately for all, Sarah was undaunted, a determined lady and a talented needlewoman who set about earning not only a living for herself and her sons but ensuring that they had an education and were put to a useful trade. Sarah worked as a seamstress, and must have been a very fine one as she often travelled abroad in this capacity with wealthy families. She has been described as a pious woman with a loving disposition, in spite of a life filled with trials and troubles. Initially the brothers were placed under the care of their Uncle Thomas who had returned to London, where he worked as a carpenter and corkcutter. Later Sarah brought them to Hull where they were educated at the Vicar's School, established in the 1730s as a charity school by the Vicar of Holy Trinity Church, where fifty to sixty boys were given free education.

Neiles and George were very different in temperament. Neiles was always thoughtful and caring, especially towards his mother whom he loved dearly; even at an advanced age he was affected emotionally when speaking of her. Both brothers had the reputation of being splendid workmen but Neiles was the steady one, George was a bit of a tearaway.

In 1839 Neiles left school, aged thirteen, and began his apprenticeship as a shipwright and joiner. Hull at this time was a rapidly expanding port. 'The Dock', opened in 1778, was a great success but was limited in that the only access was via the River Hull. It soon became impossibly congested so that the 'New Dock', accessible from the River Humber was opened in 1809, and the third, the 'Junction Dock', was brought into use in 1829, linking the other two docks and making the old town of Hull completely ringed by water. Beyond this water barrier, the houses, streets and commercial premises spread outwards to the north and west. Trade increased rapidly, stimulated by the opening of the Hull and Selby Railway in the 1840s, making easy transportation for goods from the industrial West Riding. The town was all set for prosperity.

Neiles' indenture papers have survived and they show that when he began his apprenticeship under Thomas Humphrey, Shipwright of Hull, his mother Sarah agreed to provide her son with "Meat, Drink, Washing, Lodging and Wearing Apparel during the seven years of his apprenticeship". His wages were clearly set out: 2 shillings per week for the first year and rising (but only gradually) to 7 shillings per week in the seventh year.

Evidently the brothers had inherited their mother's determination to do well and get on through education for during their training, Neiles and his brother George collected and sold bundles of kindling in order to pay for admission to the Mechanics' Institute to attend lectures and to read technical books. Family records show that eventually both brothers went to sea during their apprenticeships as ship's carpenters. They appear to have circled the world, enjoying and surviving many boisterous adventures in foreign ports.

On one shore trip in Peru, young Neiles came across the men of the Port Watch in a seafront bar, drinking heavily. It must have been a holy day as the shipmates, lurching out of the bar, bumped into a Catholic procession, wending its way down the street. Full of irreverence and the local firewater, one of their number called Mahony snatched up a nun and danced with her, twirling her round wildly, her habit flying above her knees. This outrage caused a great disturbance, ending in a running fight between the sailors and the locals in which Neiles was caught up. The fight escalated into a near riot when men of the Peruvian Naval Excise arrived to sort matters out and became involved. Unluckily for the locals, Mahony was a master of fencing and armed with a foil, he single-handedly kept back the Peruvians like Horatio defending the bridge, flicking the cutlasses out of their hands and into the hands of his comrades. But the English lads were outnumbered, the situation was becoming dangerous and they decided to run for it.

The Billany Family Tree

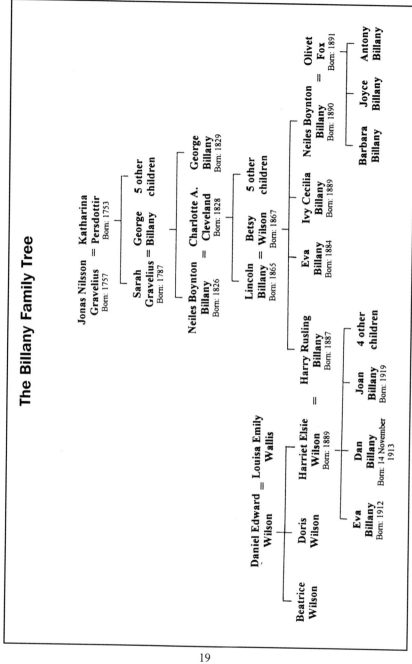

Jonas Nilsson Gravelius = Katharina Persdottir
Born: 1757   Born: 1753

Sarah Gravelius = George Billany   5 other children
Born: 1787

Neiles Boynton Billany = Charlotte A. Cleveland   George Billany
Born: 1826   Born: 1828   Born: 1829

Lincoln Billany = Betsy Wilson   5 other children
Born: 1865   Born: 1867

Eva Billany   Ivy Cecilia Billany   Neiles Boynton Billany = Olivet Fox
Born: 1884   Born: 1889   Born: 1890   Born: 1891

Barbara Billany   Joyce Billany   Antony Billany

Harry Rusling Billany =   4 other children
Born: 1887

Joan Billany
Born: 1919

Daniel Edward Wilson = Louisa Emily Wallis

Harriet Elsie Wilson =
Born: 1889

Doris Wilson

Dan Billany
Born: 14 November 1913

Eva Billany
Born: 1912

Beatrice Wilson

Neiles took the tiller of the lighter laden with the men of the Port Watch, breathless and bloody, making their way back to the ship. There was a sudden outcry when it was realised that one of the party had been left behind. Neiles thought it unwise to return to the beach in view of the bloodthirsty Peruvians lying in wait and to prevent this he withdraw the tiller from the rudder head. But the men would have none of it, they refused to abandon their colleague and threatened Neiles with violence if he would not return. So Neiles left them to it, diving overboard and swimming back to the ship standing three miles off. Through dangerous shark-haunted waters he made his way back and climbed up a rope to safety.

In 1846 Neiles completed his apprenticeship as a shipwright and carpenter. He celebrated that event by marrying seventeen year old Charlotte Cleveland at Holy Trinity Church, Hull where, almost exactly twenty years earlier, he had been baptised. One year later, he was admitted and sworn a Freeman or Burgess of the Town or Borough of Kingston upon Hull. This entitled him to certain privileges but he was also required to be "obedient to the Mayor, Aldermen and Sheriff of this Town ... and tender favour give to every Officer of this Town, in Execution of the Queen's Laws."

The young couple began their family quickly with the arrival of Emily Cleveland Billany in 1847, the first of their six children. Neiles continued to work as a shipwright, now land-based, living with his family at Botanic Terrace, Staniforth Place, in the heart of the shipping and fishing area of Hull. Lincoln, the youngest child of the family was born in 1865 and named after the U.S. President who was assassinated that year.

Neiles Boynton Billany had always taken an interest in politics. He held strong radical views, which he expressed forcefully. He supported the aims of the Chartist movement and was described as the most radical of Hull Socialists and free thinkers. He was prominent in local Trades Union activities, addressing meetings and calling for working men to support the unions then being formed for the semi-skilled and unskilled workers; the skilled men had already formed themselves into unions.

In 1885 the city of Hull was hit by election fever. Because of the Redistribution of Seats Bill, a new constituency, Hull East, was created, thus instead of the original two, the city was divided into three constituences. One of the sitting MPs, Mr C M Norwood, put himself forward as a Liberal for the Central Division, where the constituents numbered over 60,000. He was opposed by Mr H S King for the Conservatives and, in an unprecedented show of political audacity, Mr N B Billany standing as a Radical, and backed by the Hull Radical Club.

During his years as an MP for Hull, Mr Norwood, who comes over as an unappealing man, had upset many of his constituents. He had offended a local temperance group (the temperance movement was very active in Hull), the Hull Radical Club and the Hull Trades Council. The radical newspaper The Star described him in unflattering terms: "He is in appearance and manners the very embodiment of the insolence of capitalism. He is stout, well-fed and arrogant." In addition, Mr Norwood was out of favour with many of the working class Hull voters, particularly the seamen. In this city so closely connected with the sea and shipping, he had opposed Mr Plimsoll's legislation to limit cargo to a safe level; thankfully the bill had been passed without his support. Norwood's motives were to satisfy those unscrupulous ship owners who wanted to carry excessive but profitable loads. In fact he was himself a ship owner whose vessels had been singled out as overloaded by Samuel Plimsoll.

It was a hard fought election campaign and the local newspapers of the time were full of the intrigues associated with electioneering; insults flew, daggers were stabbed in backs and the columns were filled with "much excitement and bitterness of feeling". Billany was accused in a poster published by "An Indignant Elector" of splitting the Liberal vote to let in the Conservative candidate, which is exactly what did happen. He was also accused of Atheism (true, although it is understood that he attended St. James Church, where he interpreted the Christianity in the sermons as socialism), Bradlaughism (maybe) or, even Billanyism! (definitely true). Charles Bradlaugh actually visited Hull during the campaign to speak in support of Mr Billany.

Today, as then, elections are seen as exciting events, but how many present day candidates can boast of the publication of a booklet of supportive songs, to be sung at political rallies? Mr Billany could, and the following extract shows just what stirring, rabble-rousing songs they were.

For many years we've waited
For the power to elect
"One of ourselves" who knows the People's wants,
And in the House of Commons
Among the favoured and select,
Would his duty do in spite of all their taunts.

Chorus
For we have no doubt or fear
But march forward, persevere,
Neither turning to the left or to the right;
And the brighter day that's dawning,
We will hail it with a cheer
And for "Billany" the working-man we'll fight.

This and other songs appeared in Mark Hasting's "Radical Songs for Working Men, Specially Composed for Election Meetings in support of Mr N. B. Billany", which could be obtained, wholesale or retail (for one penny), from an address in George Street, Hull.

The election result showed just what Mr Billany had done by splitting the

21

Liberal vote. Mr King had won by 166 votes, polling 4193, the sitting MP, unpopular Mr Norwood, polled 4027 votes and Mr Billany the Radical, 735 votes. Although unsuccessful, Neiles Boynton Billany had certainly made an impact and it is believed that he was the first weekly waged man to stand for election to the British Parliament

The newspapers described him as a Radical but in McCalmont's Parliamentary Poll Book of British Election Results 1832-1918 he is listed as 'Labour'. These were the very early days of the Labour movement; it was not until 1893 that the Independent Labour Party was founded, in the wake of James Keir Hardie's victory on his election as Labour MP for West Ham a year earlier.

Whatever was said about Neiles Boynton Billany, all agreed that he did not lack courage and was well able to give a good account of himself. He proved he could stand up bravely to abuse from opponents, such as the time when he faced a mob who threatened to throw him in the dock, or the man who produced a knife and said, had it been night-time, he would have run it through Billany's eye. On both occasions his courage paid off and the aggressors backed down. Fifty years later, Neiles' great grandson Dan was as politically active as his 'Low Radical' ancestor could have wished. A convinced socialist and champion of working class rights, Dan was well known for arguing his viewpoint fiercely and fearlessly with all-comers.

In 1896 Neiles Boynton Billany died, mourned by friends and political foes alike as a straight dealing and straight talking man. A public subscription was raised to fund a memorial drinking fountain in his honour. A local newspaper covered the event, as follows.

The fountain is exceedingly ornamental and is made of cast iron. It is 12' in height, and will stand on a stone base about 5' square. This will be placed on a bed of concrete. The basin in the centre is supplied with four taps and cups. The whole structure is very elegant, and will form a pleasing addition to the park entrance.

It had been decided that the fountain should be placed immediately within the gates of West Park on Anlaby Road. But at the Parks Committee meeting, a snag arose.

Mr G T Hall ... pointed out that they had spent nearly all the money on the fountain and there was no surplus for the foundations. The Mayor thought it was a very modest request to make for a very useful old townsman (hear, hear) and it was resolved ... to do the work asked for at the city's expense.

During the Second World War, the fountain was hit by a vehicle during the blackout. It was damaged irreparably and later demolished.

The line of descent to Dan passes through the youngest of Neiles's children, Lincoln Billany. As a child he was a cheeky little lad, bright and very aware of it. When, aged about ten, he was given the title "Weather" for a homework essay. He offered up the following, beautifully written in copperplate handwriting:

Weather. Sir, You gave us for home lessons the subject Weather but wether you desired us to say what kind of weather, weather we were to write about a wether of sheep, wether the wether sheep liked the stormy weather, or wether the weather made the wether dissatisfied with the weather, I cannot tell wether that was the wether you wish to know about, or the weather that has been so unpleasant lately wether we like the weather or not.

A good attempt although sadly misspelled! This piece of sauce was signed "Yours respectively, Lincoln Billany", the title and signature richly embellished with scrolls and curlicues. The reaction of his teacher would have been worth watching, but his parents were proud of it and his mother kept it safely.

During the whirl of political activity surrounding the 1885 election, Lincoln was courting Betsy Wilson, the daughter of a Hull keel-owner. In October 1886 they married; he was 21, she was 19. The young couple had four children, the first boy was Harry Rusling Billany, born in 1887; their second son was named Neiles Boynton Billany after his famous grandfather. These two are Dan's father Harry and his Uncle Mick.

Lincoln had been apprenticed twice, first to a stonemason in 1879 and again in 1881 to Amos and Smith, Boilermakers of Hull. It was not usual to change trade in mid-stream but possibly he left his first apprenticeship to travel. A short article about Lincoln in the Hull Trades Council Labour Journal under the title of *Our Portrait Gallery*, states that "at an early age he took his place in the industrial struggle. He spent several months in the United States." Lincoln Billany had strong political interests, he was a socialist all his life, becoming a member of the Boilermakers' Society as soon as he was eligible and he served the Society continuously in various official positions including that of District Secretary. Although Lincoln is described in *Our Portrait Gallery* as "essentially straightforward", having "tact and good judgement", these virtues were probably restricted to his public life. At home he was a very difficult man. For so long his wife, Betsy, put up with his moods, his selfishness and his infidelities, but she was a strong-minded independent woman, and once her children were grown up, she decided she had had enough. So she divorced him. Later she remarried.

Betsy was not out of the usual mould of Hessle Road women who held the family together and watched over them with fierce maternalism. She was not close to any of her four children, except possibly her younger son, Neiles. Her daughter Eva married another Billany, a first cousin, emigrated with him to New Zealand and was completely estranged from her mother who never spoke of her again. Ivy, the other daughter, died young. Harry and his family lived locally but Betsy had little to do with them; she hardly knew the grandchildren and Harry only learned of his mother's death by letter.

The Billany side of Dan's ancestry is well documented, because of the high local profile of his grandfather and great grandfather. But it was his mother's relations who were most involved with the family during the early years.

Dan's mother was one of three sisters, Beatrice, Harriet Elsie (to give her her full name), and Doris, the daughters of Daniel Edward and Louisa Emily Wilson (née Wallis) who lived in the same area of West Hull as the Billanys. Daniel, who came from a seafaring family, died young leaving Louisa a widow with three daughters to bring up. So to support herself and her family, she took lodgers into her terraced house off Hessle Road. This was hard work with few domestic aids available even if she could have afforded them, so the three girls had to lend a hand with the chores. In the end, Louisa had to take her youngest daughter, twelve year old Doris, out of school as soon as she had passed her Labour Examination to work in the house.

Louisa had a generous, loving nature, and despite her early struggles she was always cheerful and ready to help anyone in trouble, especially one of her three beloved daughters. Together they had pulled through the hard times and they remained close when the better days came. Beatrice and Doris inherited their mother's open and friendly ways, but Elsie had a reserve about her, a coolness, which made her different from her sisters. Much later when the three girls were grown-up and independent, Louisa Wilson married for the second time. Uncle Arthur was readily accepted by the sisters and fitted into the family very well.

Chapter 5

Eva, Dan and Joan

Lincoln Billany, who considered himself to be a Working Class Intellectual, held very strong principles which he passed on to his two sons, Harry and Neiles. He was an atheist and socialist, well versed in the history of the class struggle and active in Union politics. Alongside this, he was a great believer in education. The advantage to be gained from being well read and well informed was a lesson his sons learned early in life. Both were bright boys who made the very best of their elementary school education. They attended Daltry Street School, where Harry distinguished himself by taking the class prize year after year. He stayed there until he was fourteen years old and then moved on to an apprenticeship. Neiles, three years younger, was considered to be even cleverer. He was his mother's darling and was given every opportunity to better himself. This included being entered for a Cambridge Senior Students exam, which he passed, at the age of eighteen, and then he was taken on as a pupil teacher at Wheeler Street School. Here he spent his days teaching boys only a few years younger than himself, no easy task, and when school finished, he was given extra lessons and homework by the headmaster. He stuck it for a year, and left with a very creditable report, but he had already decided there were more congenial ways of earning a living so he joined the engineering firm of Priestman's. This was just about the time that Harry, who had given up his apprenticeship for a career at sea, was courting Elsie.

Harry and his brother Neiles (in adulthood always called Mick) were totally different personalities and in later years had little contact. Nevertheless their mutual interest in music led to regular soirees in the early days. Mick played the cello in an orchestra at the Hornsea cinema, but often he brought his instrument to Devon Street for an evening of music making. They played the popular melodies of the day, favourites like *Le Poete Mourant* or *Rustle of Spring*, with Elsie on the piano and Harry on his one stringed fiddle, and anyone else joining in playing or singing. But the jolly evenings at number 73 were not regular events and the jollity was somewhat forced at times; the main performers, even the two brothers, were not really close and there were undercurrents of dislike.

As time went by they saw less and less of each other in spite of the fact that they lived only five minutes walk apart. Was there some big family bust-up? Or was it a series of petty and niggling irritations which caused a gradual estrangement? Certainly there were lots of arguments, often about politics, when the brothers, disagreeing over some fine point, would become angry and start shouting. As the children grew, their families rarely mixed. Eva, Dan and Joan hardly knew their Billany grandmother who was only a shadowy figure sometimes glimpsed sitting in the doorway of Uncle Mick's house. Joan once heard her ask, as she nodded towards them, "Are those Harry's children?" Mick's wife, Olivet, looked down on Harry Billany who tended to be uncomfortable in her company. She thought him touchy, weak and prone to sulks; he sensed her antagonism and in turn despised her 'Hessle Road' characteristics, her down-to-earth common-sense and directness. Jealousy may have played a part too, for Mick and his family lived comfortably whereas Harry had had to scrape and struggle for everything. Elsie was always civil and pleasant to her in-laws but by nature she was aloof and her misfortunes had made her even more fiercely independent, determined to do her best for her children without asking for help from anyone.

Perhaps a more simple explanation of their separateness is that the two families were both such close, self-centred units, each with three children, (both had two daughters and a son), that they tended to look inwards and to concentrate on their own family members rather than outwards to include the wider family. Certainly Harry and Mick held the same beliefs about the correct way to bring up children, both being resolved that they should be given every possible opportunity; and high on the list of their priorities came the importance of a good education.

It soon became apparent that Harry's three children were all clever. Eva was a real all-rounder, a conscientious and hardworking pupil. Dan's best subjects were spelling and learning poetry, and from an early age it was clear that Joan's talent was in art. Harry gave them every encouragement, which unfortunately sometimes took the form of sums before breakfast, not a good start to the day as he was less than patient with Joan, who was not mathematically minded. Right from the start he instilled in them all a love of books and an interest in learning for its own sake. It was a house where there was constant discussion, debate and sharing of information, an ideal learning environment for growing children. And Harry was at the centre of this. All his life he himself was an avid reader on topics ranging from philosophy, astronomy and metaphysics through to politics and poetry. But his abiding passion was politics. Like his father and grandfather, he was a staunch supporter of socialism, a strong believer in the rights of the working class and the role of the trade unions in promoting fair play for the workers. He educated his children in his beliefs, but did not indoctrinate them; his aim was to make them fully aware of their world so that then they could decide for themselves. But he wasn't stuffy; he was always full of fun and his enthusiasms were catching. They loved to go out on visits with him. One of their regular outings was to the house of William Wilberforce in the old part of the city. Wilberforce had been MP for Hull and was known as the great emancipator, working tirelessly to abolish the slave trade. The gruesome relics of slavery exhibited at the Wilberforce House Museum were a source of fascination to the young Billanys.

He also made them aware of contemporary world events, especially those with a political slant. One such was the case of Sacco and Vanzetti, two Italian Americans who in 1921 were convicted of murder. Grave doubts were raised about the fairness of the trial, many believing them to be innocent victims, persecuted because of their radical beliefs. A world-wide storm of protest followed, particularly from socialist quarters, but, in spite of new evidence, the authorities refused to grant a re-trial, and in August 1927, the two men were executed in Boston, Massachusetts. The case made a strong impression on the Billany children, especially Dan, aged thirteen. Years later, in 1938, he recalled the case in *Sonnet of Sacco and Vanzetti*, a political poem about the fight against Fascism.

Harry was an atheist but his children went to Sunday school along with all the others in the street, that was until Joan said, "Do we really have to go?" "No, of course not, if you don't want to," said Harry. So Joan and Dan gave it up there and then, although Eva continued to accompany Winnie Tanfield to church.

All three children went to Selby Street West School. It wasn't the one nearest to their home, but Harry had heard of the good reputation of this school, so from the age of five they walked the mile or so, four times a day. It accommodated both girls and boys but the two were carefully segregated, virtually into two schools, where experiences were rather different. In both, discipline was harsh, great importance being placed on Attendance, Timekeeping and Not Speaking unless asked to do so! Many of the teachers were bad-tempered and aggressive in their efforts to maintain order. In the girls' school, there was one in particular who used to spray the class with spit as she shouted at them. Her iron grey hair was cut in a bob with a side parting and held back with a grip on the left. She tore up Joan's homework, a lovingly drawn picture of Princess Ayesha, without even looking at it because Joan had spoken before the class began.

It was no surprise to anyone when at the age of eleven, Eva passed the scholarship which meant a free place at the grammar school. Both Harry and Elsie were so proud of her, determined that she should take up her place. They were not going to be put off by the cost of all the extras, such as the uniform, the books and equipment, or the fact that she would be expected to stay on at school beyond the normal leaving age of fourteen. The cousins, friends and neighbours in Devon Street were just as excited, as this was such an unusual step for one of their community. So in September 1923, while Dan and Joan returned to Selby Street West, Eva, wearing her maroon gym-slip, blazer and muffin cap, started at the Boulevard Municipal Secondary School. She was a meticulous worker, conscientiously doing her homework amid the family bustle of the living room in Devon Street, handling with ease new topics such as Latin, French and Science. The only subject where she had problems was Sport; she was clumsy and uncoordinated, just like Dan. Eva still said her prayers, particularly before an important test or exam, and it must have paid off as she passed everything with flying colours. She was ambitious, and before long had made up her mind that she would go to college and become a teacher.

The little house at Devon Street seemed to be getting smaller as the three children grew. They all shared the front bedroom, Eva and Joan in the double bed, Dan at the other side of the room, in the single. Joan, six years younger, was full of beans, very affectionate, and no doubt very irritating at times. The two sisters, one tidy and one very untidy often had rows and even came to blows on occasions, Joan inevitably coming off the worse. She was a pretty little girl, mad about roller-skating, willing to run errands for anybody so that she could whizz off on her skates. She was her mother's favourite, and Dan was her champion, always ready to take her part if there was a row. By this time Eva was growing up fast, becoming tall and somewhat remote from her brother and sister. Many of her school-friends envied her beautiful wavy hair and her flawless complexion. But Eva was more concerned with the fact that her nose was too long and determined that when she was rich (like all young people she looked on the bright side) she would have it shortened. Of course she never did. By the time she could afford it, it didn't matter any more.

Dan's days at Selby Street School were neither as happy nor as successful as Eva's. The cane was in regular use in the boys' section; learning was an obstacle course in avoiding punishment, and the aim of the teachers seemed to be to stop the boys behaving like children; every natural boyish trait was forbidden. Dan wrote feelingly about his schooldays on a number of occasions. In *Paul* he describes life in Standard Seven, the top class. The teacher is nicknamed Beaky, and his description rings so true to life that it is easy to believe he was based on Dan's own experience. In *Four o' Clock in Beaky's Classroom*, the teacher dismisses the class to a series of commands, delivered army fashion, to boys desperate to get out into the open air. Beaky, on one level, is making a game out of it, but there is a strong hint that he is enjoying wielding power, and typically there is a victim who is detained when the rest leave.

"Hands - ," one or two boys put their hands together. "Did I say put your hands together, Richmond?"
"No, sir."
"Well wait till I tell you, then, or some of you boys who are very anxious to get home will find yourselves staying till ten past four, learning to wait for the word of command."
"Yes, sir."
"Hands - together!" A short pause, whilst Beaky looked round; "eyes - closed!" Another pause. "Our Father ... "

And having rushed through The Lord's Prayer, they march out, left, right, left, right, all except Richmond who is kept back for another ten minutes.

Beaky features again, in a more sympathetic light, when he gives a lesson based on the school skull, reverently removed from the show-case for the occasion. There is no doubt that the boys are impressed with what he says.

Beaky was possessed by a faint spirit of melancholy speculation as he balanced the school skull in the palm of his hand. It was a feeling he rather liked to find in himself ...

"Please sir, whose skull was it?"

"Nobody on earth can tell you that now, Chippendale," said Beaky with a curious wistfulness which was just a shade self-consciously histrionic.

"Is it a real one, sir?"

"Yes it was once on somebody's shoulders; and whoever owned this head would have been pretty shocked if he'd been told that in the years to come a teacher would be showing his skull to a class of boys."

Contrast this with the headmaster, Old Lewis. Dan wrote this in 1938 about a type which was prevalent in boys' schools during the period of his own education.

He was a bit of a Tartar, in fact. The class of teacher from which Lewis was recruited, though it persists, is now an anachronism. It persists, because it once held education so powerfully in its grasp that the marks of its fingers take a long time to fade ... When he entered the classroom the effect of his presence was noticeable; many boys, including Paul - whom he only caned once in his life - felt a sensation of sickness, due to fear. Every boy quietly put his feet on the foot rest under his desk, and straightened his books; boys who were not working folded their arms and sat to attention; boys who were playing hid their marbles and cigarette cards, and took up their pens; boys whose hands were dirty tried surreptitiously to clean them by licking them and rubbing them on their jerseys. The whole situation, charged with sadistic fiendishness and panicky terror, was revolting and disgusting. But the type of Old Lewis lives on and triumphs.

Dan writes with compassion about his school-mates, and he goes on to describe what befell them when they grew up. Two were drowned at sea, one ended up in India trapped in the army, and two more died of tuberculosis. This is how he describes one of them in *The Trap*.

I fell in love when I was thirteen, with the boy who shared my desk at school. His name was Joey. He had very fair hair, clear blue eyes, a broad forehead, and was very good and kind ... Once during the hot weather, when Joey and I were walking home from school, he put his arm round my shoulders. It was a common enough gesture with him, in fact most schoolboys do it, without thinking: but I have remembered to this day the leaping of my heart, and all that incident is printed on my mind so that it will be clear when I'm an old man.

It would seem that Joey and Old Lewis represented the opposite ends of the spectrum.

Dan did not shine at school, and his attacks of asthma and bronchitis meant that he was frequently absent. This culminated in him spending his eleventh birthday and the subsequent weeks of November and December in Cottingham

Sanatorium. In this crisis over his health, all thoughts of the scholarship exam had been forgotten and so it was accepted that he would continue through Selby Street West School to the leaving age of fourteen. Fortunately his health began to improve, so that by the summer of 1926, still aged only thirteen, his family started to cast about looking for a suitable occupation for him.

It was Auntie Beattie who came to the rescue. She was Elsie's older sister, rather better off than the rest of the family, as she had worked her way up to become the manageress of Plummer's of Paragon Street. This was a High Class Fruit and Poultry Emporium in one of Hull's smartest shopping areas and here she was able to introduce her nephew on the bottom rung of the ladder. Dan was engaged as an errand boy at eight shillings a week, but this really meant being a dogsbody, at everyone's beck and call. At first it was an exciting step, as Dan, an undersized figure in his new suit, with an optimistic grin on his face, joined the grown-ups in the world outside the classroom. To be on friendly terms with the women working in the shop, and the men preparing the poultry and game, to join in their conversations and jokes, and to work in the bustling city centre of Hull seemed a great improvement on school. He was also surprised and indignant to see how the rich people of the city lived, how they expected their deliveries promptly and with a tug of the forelock. It was nothing to cycle several miles with just one chicken or a bunch of asparagus.

It did not take long for Dan's enthusiasm to wear off. Deliveries were made either by box-bicycle, a wobbly, arm-aching experience controlling the heavy box on the front of the machine as one steered through narrow streets, or worse still, by handcart, this for the really heavy loads. Dan was neither strong enough, nor committed enough to cope with such hard physical work, so he tried to keep out of the way, seeking refuge in the cellar, bagging up vegetables and listening to the gossip of the men. In *Paul*, he describes his experiences delivering, first by bicycle,

> It was a raw, cold November morning, and this made his lungs feel uneasy. The bicycle he was riding was a painful instrument; the iron frame-work of the saddle had come through the leather, and it jarred and jolted into his flesh the more efficiently since the tyres were solid. There were no handlegrips on the bars, and he could feel the coldness of the iron through his worn gloves.

And then with the handcart,

> Paul took the handcart and resignedly pushed the creaking load through the streets to the back door of the Royal Hotel. He was slight for his age, and when he had carried a four stone bag of turnips through to the kitchen, he was exhausted, and leaned on the wall for a minute or two to recover his breath. The Royal had a large staff of women in the kitchen, and they had always adopted a motherly attitude to Paul.
> "Poor little bugger has all he can manage wi' them bags o' swedes."

"Your chest's bad again today, son, isn't it?"

"Yes," said Paul, "it's the fog this morning; I'm always like it when its foggy."

"I wonder they don't send somebody wi' you, to help you to unload the stuff."

Paul tried not to look like a martyr, but he felt like one; he basked demurely in the sympathy of the women. He went back to the handcart and returned with more vegetables; a crate of cabbages, about twice as big as himself.

"What's it you've got, asthma or bronchitis?" asked one of the women.

"Both," said Paul, with perfect truth and a certain amount of pride, abstractly pitying himself. But this was too much for the women, who suspected him, reasonably enough, of trying to claim more than his share of misfortune; and they laughed good-naturedly, and knew him after that as "The little kid with Both."

Another aspect of the job which carried an awful fascination for Dan was the killing room. This was where the chickens were killed, plucked and dressed ready for the customer. Dan describes his first experience there, again as Paul.

Paul had never killed chickens, but had watched with fascination and some horror the operation as performed by the others. He had always even from quite early childhood, felt strong scruples about hurting or killing animals, since he seemed to have a marked capacity for identification, and, when he saw someone tread on a beetle, he himself felt in imagination the crushing agony of its death; also he felt that an injustice had been committed. But with regard to chickens, he had to admit that he himself very much enjoyed eating them; therefore it was only right he should be prepared to kill them.

(This last statement is typical of Dan Billany who never shirked from doing what he saw as his duty, however unpalatable the task might be). Paul approaches the cage to extract a chicken, but it escapes and there follows a frantic chase round the cellar until Robert, an old hand at the game, catches the bird.

It was like a Chaplin film, Robert creeping quietly up on the clucking, beady-eyed chicken, which allowed him to come within three feet of it and then fled squawking, with its wings and claws whirling. But there was also a touch of the macabre in the fact that, absurd as the chase seemed, it did actually mean death to the chicken.

Dan's Auntie Beattie, manageress of the shop, kept a watchful eye on everybody including her nephew. "What did you have for dinner?" she would ask him every afternoon. "Bread and jam," Dan would always reply with a grin. In fact Beattie's interest in the family helped them out on many occasions. Back in the early 1920s, when Harry was desperately looking for employment, she fixed up short periods of seasonal work for him in the shop. He must have been a cut above the ordinary worker, because Frank Plummer wrote in his testimonial that he was "an artisan with ability of a very refined nature." Beattie often called in at Devon Street on her way home from work. It is not difficult to imagine the scene:

"Now Elsie love, how are you feeling this week?" It is Saturday tea-time and Auntie Beattie has arrived, muffled up against the raw night in her fur collared tweed and bearing the usual string-handled carrier which she places upon the table. "And look what I've got for my three favourite bairns!"

The bag is pounced upon by Eva, Dan and Joan who leap up to meet their aunt as she steps in off the street. Whilst the children examine its contents, slightly damaged pears, russet apples, silver wrapped tangerines and spotty bananas, Beattie scans her sister's face with concern. Then she remembers the other parcel and passes it over to Elsie. "Thought this might come in useful," she says. "It's too small for me now."

Elsie gently shakes out a beautifully cut black crepe dress, embroidered in bold horizontal patterns. "Oh how lovely," she says, holding the garment against herself, her face looking very white next to the black material. Joan leaves the fruit to her brother and sister and approaches her mother with awe.

"Mam, its beautiful!" she whispers as she buries her face in the soft cloth, still faintly scented with Auntie Beattie's perfume.

Beattie was the eldest of the three Wilson sisters. Her husband, Clarence, had been killed in the First World War after only six months of marriage, so she moved in with the third sister, Doris, who lived with her husband and family in a large house at 307 Spring Bank West. Later they were joined by their mother, when she was widowed for the second time. They always maintained good relations with Dan's family. Grandma Wilson visited Devon Street every Thursday, and Beattie and Doris regularly came down to play bridge, bringing their own bottle of gin, and a couple of Frank Plummer's oranges to squeeze into it. (Elsie looked on disapprovingly; she didn't hold with alcohol). Doris had two daughters, Eileen and Molly. They were younger than the Billany children and looked up to their cousins with awe, they seemed so clever, so confident and ambitious.

★★★

One of the things Dan enjoyed about the male company at Plummer's was the political discussions in the cellar. He had been well schooled in socialism by his father, and with the confidence of youth, butted into the conversation with very firmly expressed opinions. Whatever he lacked in physical capabilities, he more than made up for by his gift of the gab. He spoke with passion about those subjects which moved him, and he got away with it, partly because he was so articulate, but also because he had a witty and humorous way with words to mitigate the seriousness of his arguments. This was a good training ground for Dan Billany, the political speaker, and of course Dan Billany, the writer. However his days as an errand boy were numbered. An apprenticeship seemed to be the next obvious step if he were going to get on in life.

Chapter 6

Wider horizons

It was in 1929, when he was 16 years old, that Dan became an apprentice electrician with Humber Electrical Engineering. As the newest recruit, he was put to menial jobs: tea-making, fetching and carrying for the tradesmen, sweeping up in the shops, altogether not much improvement on his lowly status at Frank Plummer's. Time passed and he began to learn the jargon and the basic processes of electrical wiring. At last he felt that he was being accepted into the adult world of work, leaving boyhood behind, especially when he was allowed to act as assistant to the qualified men in the workshops and, more interestingly, on outside contracts in the town.

As a requirement of his apprenticeship, Dan had to undertake at least three years study at evening classes, the first year of which was a foundation course in technical subjects. It was so different from school which he had passed through unmemorably, where only the poetry and English lessons came anywhere near to touching him. Here at the Technical College the tutors were worlds away from the 'Beaky' type; here they regarded their students as intelligent young men, eager to learn. In this atmosphere, Dan flourished.

It wasn't easy at first. It was two years since Dan had been in a classroom, although he had carried on reading and extending his fields of interest. The night classes became important to him; what had started as a duty became more of a pleasure and a challenge to do well. An indication of his level of commitment is his one hundred per cent attendance in the first year. A certificate dated July 1930 shows Dan taking first place in all the four subjects in which he was examined: Technical Drawing, General Elementary Science, Calculations and English.

In the early days of Dan's employment, his firm won a contract to modernise the electrical wiring in Hammonds, one of Hull's largest department stores. Working alone one day on the lighting for the shop windows, Dan noticed a pile of ladies' gloves, apparently left over from the display. Dan was tempted and just before leaving for the night, stuffed a pair of the soft leather gloves into his toolbag. Back home, his mother was so surprised and delighted by her unexpected gift that Dan, rather shamefacedly, confessed how he had come by it. The family was shocked at so uncharacteristic an action on Dan's part, but after much discussion agreed that it would be impractical to return the stolen gloves. Dan was unmoved by the fuss. Possibly he felt that his mother deserved a nice pair of gloves just as much as any rich lady of the town. Or maybe it was a genuine mistake and he thought they were going to be thrown out. In any case, the matter was dropped and soon forgotten by all except eleven-year-old Joan, who for many weeks trembled in fear at every knock, expecting the open door to reveal a policeman, threatening to drag her brother up before the Magistrates. It did not happen. Elsie kept the gloves and wore them for long afterwards.

The late 1920s and early 1930s saw the boundaries of Hull fanning out rapidly as new private and council-owned estates were planned and built. Also at this time many of the older properties of Hull were undergoing the change from gas to electric power. In his novel *Paul*, Dan describes how two men, one an old school chum of Paul's are sent by their firm to install electricity in a decrepit old house divided into one-room flats. A queer smell puzzles one of the young electricians.

In one of the lower rooms, when Arthur was taking up a floor-board, to get at which they had had to move a bed and lift a sheet of cheap canvas, the queer disinfectanty small became even stronger.

Then Arthur's mate said, "Look here." Arthur looked, and saw a reddish-brown creature walking across the floor.

"What is it?"

"Bug."

"Christ!" said Arthur shivering with disgust. His mate flattened the insect with a tap of his hammer, and they went on working, crawling under beds very gingerly. They found, when they came to cut skirting boards or disturb wallpaper that the house was riddled with bugs. The property, being old, verminous, and decayed, should have been destroyed. Instead it was being fitted with electric light. In each room which once had been only a part of the life of a family, now a family lived altogether, stewing in its squalor and dirt and misery. The staircases and landing were public places which it was no one's care to keep clean.

During his time with Humber Electrical Dan saw many such scenes and worked in similar conditions. How could he help but compare the bug-ridden flats whose pathetic inhabitants took pride in offering the workmen cups of tea, with the comfortable homes where he had delivered fruit and vegetables, on Plummer's box bicycle? The contrasting worlds he had read about in socialist literature and heard about from his father were now vividly real to him; the theory had turned into fact. Contact with the disgusting conditions in which many people existed made Dan determined to spread his radical views by whatever means he could. In the evening after work, when the tea things had been cleared away, Dan and his father settled down to political discussion. Harry's was the rational, thoughtful voice of middle age, bringing the experience and disappointments of a lifetime into the argument; Dan's was the idealistic voice of youth, seeing everything in black and white, with none of the grey shades of disillusionment that time allows to creep in.

During the second year of his apprenticeship, Dan continued to attend evening classes at the Technical College and again found success. In July 1931 he achieved first place in two of his three subjects, but he dropped back to second class in his major subject, Electrical Engineering. This appears to be the point where he began to lose interest in completing his apprenticeship, but what could he find to take its place?

Dan decided to leave Humber Electrical Engineering; he could not see himself spending the rest of his life as an electrician. He and the manager, Mr Raahauge, had found it impossible to work together. The manager was not used to articulate young men with radical leanings spreading what he saw as anarchy and unrest amongst the workforce. Dan, fervent socialist and debater, was not used to keeping quiet if he thought something needed to be said. The situation became increasingly uncomfortable until Dan handed in his notice, which was speedily accepted. It was a serious step to leave an apprenticeship, as Harry Billany knew well. He had done it himself but he did not condemn his son, as others might have done, though Harry felt some dismay that Dan should so easily cast aside the chance of a secure future.

It was lucky for Dan that the Billany family were so supportive. Here he was, nearly eighteen years old with no job, no qualifications and, worst of all, no real idea of what he wanted to do. He knew what he *didn't* want to do; his experiences in the retail and the electrical trade had shown him that. But it was not easy to walk into a well paid, satisfying job, however clever you were. The Depression was starting to bite, jobs were scare and sought after by men with far more training then he had. All attempts to find the right position ended in failure; meanwhile he was earning nothing, being kept by his family, who had only just pulled themselves up from poverty to a decent standard of living. Eventually he hit rock bottom, admitted defeat and applied for the dole. But money was not handed out anything like as freely as today; Dan was means tested and told he was ineligible for the dole because there was already a wage earner in the house and his sister was receiving an education grant. Desperately in need of money, he decided to try door-to-door selling. The product was wireless sets, very desirable, high quality wireless sets, as Dan described them on countless doorsteps. It was hard going, even for a young man with a persuasive vocabulary, friendly smile and trustworthy appearance. It seemed that those households prosperous enough to buy a set had one already and the rest, eager enough to purchase, had barely sufficient income to cover necessities. It did not take long for Dan to realise he was wasting his time.

At this point he should have been at a very low ebb but he was not dejected. During the long days walking the streets of Hull, he had been sorting out his ideas and had come to the conclusion that the best, in fact the only route for him was to go ahead with further education. So his next step was to enrol at the free study classes for the unemployed which were held at the Technical College. Although still hazy about his final goal, he knew he had found the right direction at last. Jim Tanfield, his boyhood friend, says that Dan "renounced the world and returned to school".

This led to full-time study at the Technical College in the autumn of 1931, where his outstanding ability had already caught the attention of the Principal, Mr Percy Bates. On the strength of this he was offered a free place in the daytime classes. After discussion with his family and with the example of Eva before him, he had decided to study for matriculation. This was the fore-runner of the General Certificate of Education, but at that time a student had to pass every one of a whole range of subjects in order to qualify. To start with, Dan attended the Park Street premises of the Technical College, steadily working his way through such new subjects as Inorganic and Physical Chemistry, Physics and French.

In order to qualify, Dan also needed to pass English, Maths and a foreign language, so in addition to his daytime work, he attended the evening matriculation classes in these subjects at the College of Commerce in Brunswick Avenue. The Principal, Allan George, accepted him on Percy Bates' recommendation and granted him free tuition. Possibly both men felt sorry for this penniless lad trying to better himself, but their faith in him was soon justified when it became obvious that this was a young man of outstanding ability and determination. Allan George recalls this time in a letter written to Dan on 3rd October 1940.

I have just looked up your record as an evening student here, and can see, as I have often said to others about you, that your progress in French and Latin was remarkable. You will probably remember the first interview you had with me when Bates sent you along as a somewhat raw youth wanting to begin a foreign language, mathematics, and later, Latin. Not fully appreciating the material of which you are made, I and others wondered at first whether you would be able to reach your goal. However, after a time, Ableson, Mrs Preston and others all said that Dan Billany was a marvel.

In the common-room of the Technical College students met regularly to discuss everything under the sun. Here Dan made two good friends, both of whom in different ways were to have an important influence on him. They were Reg Bloomfield and Leo Peters.

The spring of 1932 saw another change in the lives of the Billany family. Harry and Elsie had, for some time, been planning to make a move from Devon Street; they needed more space for their growing family than the cramped sham-four could offer. For years they had had their names down on the council housing list but, until now, they were doubtful whether they could afford the rent on the sort of house that Elsie had set her heart on. But now Harry had a regular job on the trams, Eva, aged nineteen, had almost completed her teacher training at the College on Cottingham Road; Dan, just turned eighteen was settled into his studies and Joan, twelve years old, was in her first year at the Boulevard Secondary School, having won a scholarship just as Eva had done some years earlier. Taking everything into consideration, it seemed to be the ideal time and so when they were offered a house, they made the move to 15 Lakeside Grove.

The new house was on the recently built council estate just across Hessle Road at Gipsyville, that same site which Dan and his pals had used as an adventure playground during the building activities. Although not far from their previous home, it seemed like another world. It was a semi-detached house, fully electric with big airy rooms, a garden front and back, and it had a real bathroom with hot water and toilet. There were three bedrooms, so Dan was able to have a room of his own, and there were two sitting rooms downstairs. They had money to spare for the first time and Elsie was determined that they were going to get off to a good start. The house was re-decorated throughout before they moved in and they bought new furniture: for the back room, a leather three piece suite and a wooden dining table with barley twist legs, and for the front room, a grey moquette suite. A rural scene sketched by Dan hung on one wall and a painting by Eva on another. Elsie was so proud of it all. She insisted that the 'Cook-and-Heat' stove in the kitchen was removed. This was an ugly black coal-fired contraption designed to be a cooker, water-heater and also to feed some radiators. Elsie said that it was inefficient and in its place had an all-electric system installed, a cooker in the kitchen and log-effect fires in the two other rooms. Harry made a grill to fit over the living-room fire so that a pan of food could be kept warm on top of it. But in the first few weeks of that warm spring, a fire was not necessary and Elsie arranged a big bowl of daffodils in the hearth.

This was the sort of home that Elsie had dreamed of during the previous twenty years of her marriage. The worries of poverty, separation, successive pregnancies and infant deaths had made it seem as if her hopes would never be realised; now at last she had her wishes fulfilled and the family could look forward to the most settled and carefree period of their life. And to complete the family circle, it was at about this time that they acquired Bonzo, a brown mongrel dog of great character. Bonzo's face appears in family snaps, he received regular mention in letters and Dan wrote about him affectionately on a number of occasions. This description is from *The Trap*.

> Bonzo suddenly burst into the garden and hurtled up the lawn, a brown ball of a dog, to fling himself on me, barking with joy, leaping, licking, seizing my wrist and mumbling it with mimic ferocity but never letting his strong teeth grip - prancing on his hind legs, fore legs stiff out in front of him, ears laid back, eyes alive with joy - he ... came at me again and again, his jaws laughing with delight.

At this stage, one can clearly see Dan, the young man emerging from Dan, the boy. Without exception his contemporaries describe him as a lovely person, who never said an unkind word about anyone, (barring Hitler and other fascist tyrants). He was fun to be with. His appealing sense of humour and clever turn of phrase made him entertaining company whatever the circumstances - in serious political discussions just as much as on social and family occasions. And one could rely on Dan. His even-tempered, optimistic nature made him an anchor, someone to whom his family and friends could turn knowing he would sort out the problem. An early illustration of this occurred soon after they had moved into Lakeside Grove.

One Sunday afternoon Joan, aged twelve, had gone out for a walk with a school-friend called Mary. The rest of the family were at home and were shocked when sometime later, Mary arrived back flushed and breathless, to tell them that Joan had gone off with a strange man. Harry was called in from the garden, Dan from his studies in the front room and together they made Mary recount every detail of the story. The two girls had met a man with a little puppy on a piece of string. Joan had immediately stopped to fondle the puppy who was very friendly and licked her face. The man was friendly too and allowed her to lead the puppy on its string, so she joined him in his walk. This was all Mary could tell them as she had then taken fright and run home.

At this point Elsie panicked and decided the police must be called, so Eva was dispatched to the station on Hessle Road and returned before too long with a young policeman. Mary did her best to describe the man but she couldn't remember much except that he wore a hat; she gave them a better description of the puppy. Dan and the constable were just leaving to search the neighbourhood when Joan sauntered in, completely unaware of the panic. Anxious cross-questioning revealed that she had indeed gone for a walk with a strange man. Nothing much had happened except that he had persuaded her to let him kiss her in a phone box! Both parents erupted at this but Dan calmed them down. The stranger had told her his name was Jimmy and she had agreed to go to the pictures with him the following evening. Joan found it hard to understand what all the fuss was about and why her mother was so cross with her. Meanwhile Dan and the rest of the family were in conference and a plan was hatched to trap the stranger.

Next day, outside the Eureka Cinema Joan waited for him. When he arrived, he asked her to wait a little longer while he went into a nearby barber's for a shave. The tension rose and then, as he emerged from the shop, Dan came up behind him and tapped him on the shoulder. "Excuse me, this is my sister," he said, with quiet menace in his voice. The policeman and Elsie and other interested parties converged from doorways and alleys to surround the man, who was by now extremely shaken. Some discussion followed but eventually the general concensus, led by Dan, was to let him off.

Although this period of the thirties was a hard time for many people with unemployment spiralling, the failure of heavy industry and consequent strikes, and the threat of Nazism looming on the continent, yet for the Billanys it was a time of optimism. The family fortunes were on the up and up. Already they owned an AJS motorcycle and sidecar which meant that all five of them could take a trip into the country on a Sunday or visit the local seaside resorts. Harry drove the bike with Dan on the pillion, whilst Elsie and the two girls travelled in the sidecar, one behind the other sheltered by a celluloid windscreen.

Occasionally Dan would ride the AJS himself, taking Jim Tanfield along as passenger. Jim declined to ride pillion, preferring what he thought was the safety of the sidecar. Dan's love of speed and excitement made him a reckless driver and on one occasion the more cautious Jim, seated alone in the sidecar became concerned. "How fast are we going Dan?" he called out as they raced along the road to Cottingham. "Only forty, you worry too much!" laughed Dan and opened her up even more. Jim was convinced that the sidecar was working loose, juddering and swinging away from the bike. When they got back home, Dan knelt down to examine it and with one touch, the connecting bolt sheared and the sidecar slumped to the ground. Jim was horrified and thoroughly alarmed to think what a lucky escape he had had. He said, "What if ...?" several times, but Dan laughed it off, it was just a bit of fun to him and after all, no-one had been hurt. As soon as they could afford it, Harry sold the AJS and bought a car, a Standard Eight with a fabric body. There was no garage at Lakeside Grove, so a section of the garden fence was hinged and made into a gate, to make car-parking space. All three Billany children learnt to drive in the Standard. In the thirties, owning and driving a car was unusual, particularly for working class people, and it was an exciting step which appealed greatly to Dan. It meant independence and gave the driver status, even if he had to admit that the car belonged to his father. The Billanys, always modern in their outlook, also encouraged the two girls to drive at a time when daughters were often resigned to the passenger seat.

In the field of fashion Dan was sorting out his ideas. He liked clothes to be well-made, and was particular about the quality and the cut of the cloth. A snapshot of this time shows Dan, accompanied by Bonzo, lying on the lawn at Lakeside Grove supported on one elbow, in a theatrically negligent pose. His 'bounder and cad' style of dress consists of a spectacular pair of plus-fours and loudly checked knee socks. In his surroundings as well as his dress Dan was experimenting in design and taste. Now that he no longer had to share a bedroom with his sisters he could indulge in any decorative scheme which took his fancy. The result was an austere affair, like a monk's cell: a polished wood floor covered in black mats and black painted dressing-table, made by Harry. However appealing this cell might be, there was no form of heating, so during the winter evenings he spent little time in it, preferring to study in the quiet and warmth of the front room downstairs.

There was plenty of studying to be done. In addition to his day time classes at the Technical College and his night school at the College of Commerce, Dan was expected to work on his own and undertake extensive reading. His interest in literature had begun at an early age, encouraged by his father's insistence on the importance of reading, and it was about this time that he started writing himself, mainly poetry or short stories, and letters to the Hull Daily Mail on political topics.

Dan had been brought up with music all around him. Elsie was a fine pianist and the whole family enjoyed listening to the wireless and gramophone records.

But from his early teens Dan's taste began to vary from that of his parents and sisters. Harry and Elsie preferred the popular classics whilst Joan, still only a young girl, naturally loved the ballads and crooners of the day. Dan's father gathered together an informal string trio whose activities were confined to the front room at Lakeside Grove, which rang shrilly with the music of light operettas and tunes from musical shows. Along with Harry on his one-stringed fiddle there was Uncle Mick on the 'cello and another friend, Harry Monaghan, on the violin. The rest of the family, who poked fun at Harry's musical preferences, withdrew to the back room and let them get on with it. Dan, in his determined way, had taught himself to play the piano, but although he had mastered the mechanics of the instrument and learned to read music, he was never a dextrous player nor relaxed enough to make a success of it. Probably he demanded too high a standard of himself, judging his playing against that of the professional pianists on his gramophone records.

However, uninfluenced by his family or friends, Dan's views on music began to emerge. Maybe he had heard classical recitals on the wireless which appealed to him; perhaps he felt in some way that an interest in classical music matched his passion for abstruse literature. Whatever the reason, he seemed to be going out of his way to be different. As soon as he could afford it, he started a classical record collection which included favourites such as Tauber, Caruso and Clara Butt. In his friendship with Reg Bloomfield he found a fellow enthusiast, they were regulars in the audience at the Hull City Hall, which attracted performers of international reputation like Galli-Curchi and John McCormack.

Dan and Reg were also keen theatregoers whenever time and money permitted. They enjoyed equally the serious and dramatic productions of writers like Galsworthy on the one hand and on the other, a Ben Travers farce such as *Rookery Nook*. Dan's memory was so good that he could store up whole passages of dialogue from the plays and recreate the action, just as he had done on cinema visits, on the way back home. There were times when he entertained a tram full of passengers with his funny voices and jokes. It seemed he enjoyed being in the limelight.

Chapter 7

From a soap box

At the corner of King Edward Street outside the Co-operative Stores a small crowd is gathered. Dan aged eighteen, bare-headed and heedless of the cold December weather, is visible head and shoulders above them because he is standing on a wooden crate. In his left hand is a bunch of papers, but he does not need to refer to notes. His strong voice carries well and the onlookers stare at him with stolid expressions.

"... Don't listen to what they tell you about nationalisation. Nationalisation! What a ring it has to it, but do you know what it means? What it will mean to everyone of you - you, the working men who form the backbone of our country? It's nothing but a conspiracy of the captains of industry, a national pact to oppress the workers still further! State capitalism! That's all it is and if Commander Kenworthy, our illustrious MP, were to have his way, he would have you believing that this is all part of a socialist programme. What nonsense. No true socialist ever advocated state capitalism.

"What's more, if the Commander is a socialist, why does he make political capital out of the sayings of Jesus Christ? Does he think that the basis of socialism is the same as Christianity? - Let me tell you what socialism really means ... "

★★★

Dan's comrade-in-arms during this period of intense political activity was Leo Peters, a fellow student at the Technical College. By this time Dan had entered on a course of full-time study and his sights were set on going up in the world, even making a political mark. When he met Leo, they immediately hit it off. Both had come to education through free classes for the unemployed; both were intelligent young men, avid readers, earnest debaters, keen to change the world. Each fed off and encouraged the other and they became committed socialists, with strong communist leanings. Together they joined the Labour League of Youth, which had its headquarters in Freehold Street, later they became members of the Socialist Party of Great Britain.

Although they came from very different backgrounds, both had been brought up as socialists, and both were fired to share their views and ambitions for society with anyone who would listen. Soap-box oratory was their starting point. Together at first, and then separately, they took their stand on street corners and preached to audiences ranging from two small boys and a dog to crowds of up to a hundred. Heckling and abuse they took in their stride, countering and relishing it.

Dan with his shock of curly hair, forceful personality, and gift of the gab attracted a lot of attention on his soap-box. Not only was he a good speaker, adopting just the right tone, but he had a firm grasp of the facts and a real evangelical zeal to convert his listeners to what he was convinced was the truth. He was genuinely angry at the unfairness of life and not only sympathised with the under-privileged, but felt it his duty to do something about it. Communism seemed to have all the answers. It was an extension of the socialist principles on which he had been raised, and also it was a fashionable intellectual pursuit of the period. Dan, with his developing interest in the world around him, was immediately attracted by it.

Here Dan describes, somewhat tongue-in-cheek, his friend Leo's platform style. He appears as Felix La Roche in Dan's unpublished novel *A Season of Calm Weather*.

Felix was much the better speaker, despite an unpromising appearance; he was short, a little fat, slightly bow-legged, flat-footed and very short-sighted, which caused him to peer closely at any papers he happened to be quoting from; he was always spotty. He was very poor and lived on fish and chips. In speaking he concentrated on not being subtle, on avoiding any strain on the mentality of his hearers, and on making everything childishly simple; he took it for granted that his audience was half-witted. This ensured his success with the British working class.

Their career as street corner preachers went from strength to strength. Dan got a real kick out of handling the crowd, his strong voice, quick sense of humour and ability to hold people's attention were a recipe for success and he loved it. Taking a risk was all part of the excitement, facing aggression and shouting down the hecklers; his great-grandfather, Neiles Boynton Billany, would have been proud of him. Even so there were times when he had to pick up his box and make a run for it!

His sisters and some of his friends were shocked and alarmed by this new found passion, afraid he would be arrested and dragged off to prison. Not so Harry who was openly pleased at the remarkable way his son was developing. Dan laughed off all objections and continued as before. Unemployment, the iniquities of the benefit system and means test, the relative merits of socialism and communism, national and world affairs, injustices and incompetencies of all kinds; these were the issues that Dan and Leo debated on the streets of Hull.

Both were very well read, fully in command of their facts, with a conviction that they knew what was right. A flavour of Dan's style can be gauged from the letters he wrote to the Hull Daily Mail; this one was published in January 1932, shortly after his eighteenth birthday.

... Before India was annexed by Britain, productive activity was a pot pourri of arts, crafts and slavery. At the onset of British rule, first Clive and then Hastings acted as extortionists, and the millions of money which these men wrung from the natives have become famous - or infamous. The torrent of wealth which they released from India has never abated; to this day it is increasing ...

Needless to say, the small native boss looked longingly on this blood money of England's. He started the "India for Indians" campaign that has since steadily grown in volume. Mr Gandhi, feted and feasted by native capitalists, carries on with the good work of rousing the Indian wage-slaves to shake off a white vampire to be sucked dry by a brown one ...

The articulate, ironic expression, and the underlying passion in what he is saying would be more appropriate to a mature politician than to a young man just embarking on his first course of serious study. His knowledge and understanding are exceptional too, and his views typically controversial.

The early 1930s was a period of high unemployment throughout the country, and especially so in Hull where the dock workers were very badly hit. At this time each local council was responsible for administering benefit, and Hull was particularly short of cash. At the year end, March 1932, the Public Assistance Committee had overspent their budget for out-relief (the only form of welfare payment) by more than £30,000. There was much unrest in the city manifested in angry meetings and demonstrations. Later nation-wide marches caught the headlines in a much more dramatic way, but on January 7th 1932, there was an unprecedentedly high turn-out in Hull in a protest against the means test and the proposed reduction in out-relief. Dan and Leo were part of the thousand strong crowd which assembled on Corporation Field, and after a rousing address by their leaders, proceeded to march through the city centre to the Guildhall in the hopes of putting their requests to the Council which was in session there. They had almost reached their goal when the police confronted them by the Post Office and gently but firmly ordered them back. There was muttering but no arguing, no violence, and gradually the assembly dispersed. However, they did make the front page of the Hull Daily Mail where their demands were clearly reported, so it was not a failure.

Dan and Leo liked to make a bit of a splash on marches and demonstrations and often brandished a pair of battered antique halberds which Leo's Jewish father had brought with him from Russia, when he had fled the country in 1900. He had been an important man, court photographer at St Petersburg, and had managed to escape with various antiques and valuables, including jewellery and signed photographs of the Tsar and his family. In England he married and set up photographic studios in Scarborough, Leeds, London and Hull, but by the time Dan knew him, his wife had left him, his businesses had collapsed and he and Leo lived above his disused studio at 59 Whitefriargate, in the old part of the city. He was called Peter Peters, but this was the name he had been given by the immigration authorities when he had arrived in Britain. They dismissed his unpronounceable Russian name, and adapted his first name into a surname as well. Dan was delighted to know a real Russian, especially such an eccentric one. He describes him in *A Season Of Calm Weather*.

> Customers never came and the rent was never paid. Sometimes old La Roche would walk softly through the dusty studio, with a faded, apologetic air, as if he thought the landlord might hear him if he were noisy, and the dust might rise if he were not circumspect. He was a slightly built man with black hair and a black beard, mild, nervous eyes, and a foreign accent. In all the time that Philip knew him, he only once went out of the house; that was one afternoon, when Felix took him to the pictures.

The socialist scene in Hull revolved round a whole series of small societies and leagues, generally in conflict with each other and the main Labour Party. Dan and Leo joined the Socialist Party of Great Britain but were both expelled for various infringements. By this time, Leo had met his future wife, Mary, and together they set up a Hull branch of the Communist Party in 1932. Dan never joined the Party although he called himself a communist. He was certainly very familiar with their policies and he loved to argue and debate with them. Generally their meetings took the form of discussions in somebody's house and Dan was often invited as he could be relied on to spice up the argument. He once took Jim Tanfield to such a meeting in Grosvenor Street, where Jim was bewildered by the conversation, ("The word 'proletariat' seemed to come up in every sentence!") and saddened by the fact that when the lady of the house brought in sandwiches and cakes for supper, they all scoffed them without even noticing what they were eating, or offering her a word of thanks.

During the thirties, awful years of world-wide depression, communism had a great appeal. It seemed to have the answer both to wide scale unemployment and poverty, and to the rising threat of fascism. And in Russia, communism appeared to be doing such an admirable job. Influential visitors from the West, such as G B Shaw, C Day Lewis and Rex Warner were completely convinced by what they saw - a flourishing economy with a happy workforce. Dan was no more aware of the truth than they were, but nevertheless he declined to join the Communist Party. Perhaps he was put off by the bickering, the endless and fruitless arguing over details, the going-round-in-circles that he encountered at meetings. He was aware of the gulf between idealism and reality and the shortcomings of his fellow communists, constantly squabbling with each other. (Leo himself was later expelled from the Communist Party, the excuse being that he had amassed an arsenal of weapons - these were the antique Russian halberds!) Dan's views are expressed unequivocally in *A Season of Calm Weather*.

> You Communists, collecting members as a kid collects stamps, gradually hypnotise yourselves into believing the arguments you use to get them, and particularly you get into the way of taking it for granted that the political fight is the only one - a view which is directly contrary to the official one of your party, and contrary to that of Marx. The Communist Party is only of real importance in that it provides an organisation which is preparing for revolution, in contradistinction to all other parties which are based on the hypothesis that the present system is going to last.

One off-shoot of the Communist Party which attracted a great deal of support was the National Unemployed Workers' Movement. By 1932 it had a membership of 50,000, Dan and Leo among them. It was this organisation that was responsible for a series of hunger marches ending in London, and attracting enormous sympathy from all who saw them pass by. Dan and Leo did their bit by agitating for benefit reform by distributing leaflets and posters, and persuading shop-keepers to allow them to display in their windows names, addresses and photographs of the people on the Benefit Committee.

Dan's reluctance to join the Communist Party may have been because life was opening up for him in so many directions that he just didn't have the time or commitment to devote himself exclusively to politics. Suddenly everything seemed to be happening. He was inspired by the new academic subjects he was discovering and the realisation that he was 'university material'. Then there was his writing, his interest in music and theatre and his widening circle of friends. He never wavered in his political views, but he also kept his feet firmly on the ground and continued studying hard at the Technical College, his sights fixed on an academic career. Leo matriculated, on his second attempt in 1932 and embarked on a science course at Hull University. Dan continued working towards his matriculation and in 1933 gained a first division pass in English, French, Mathematics, Economics and Physics, with distinctions in English and French. His family swelled with pride when the results were announced. Harry bragged about it to everyone, Elsie was more reticent, but both were fully behind Dan, convinced of his potential and determined to do all they could to support him. His sisters were equally thrilled, but not surprised; Eva had watched him with admiration as he overtook her, and Joan thought her big brother was a genius.

Dan's passion was English Literature, particularly poetry, and he had a huge store of memorised verse, some of it from his elementary school days. His taste was wide-ranging including Pope, Wordsworth, Hardy, Yeats, Auden, but he tended towards the romantic. Besides this he read everything he could lay his hands on, covering the broadest spectrum, and he absorbed it all, helped by his phenomenally good memory.

Dan and Leo were now seeing less of each other, but there were occasional chance encounters in the town when they would easily slip into a conversation started maybe months before. Dan applied to Hull University to read English Literature but was shocked to discover that to be eligible for this course he had to reach matriculation standard in Latin. This was a completely new subject, but he was not to be put off, having come so far. He spent the next year at home teaching himself Latin, and with the help of another College of Commerce free night class, he passed. It also meant that he had the leisure to do some sustained writing, and he was able to pursue his interest in economics. With its close political links this subject had always held a fascination for him and he was allowed to attend Dr Roll's university classes as an extra-mural student. Erich Roll, later Lord Roll, author of *A History of Economic Thought*, was Leo's economics tutor, so possibly it was through his influence that Dan got this opportunity.

The next problem to be faced was money. Even with the full support of his parents Dan was not going to be able to go through university without considerable financial help so he started applying for grants and bursaries. On the recommendation of Percy Bates and Allan George, he had already been awarded £50 from the Riley-Luxton Foundation for the year spent working at home, but the future looked pretty precarious unless he could secure financial backing for the next three years; at university he would have to pay tuition fees, and books and equipment would not be cheap. There followed months of tedious filling in of forms, in which every detail of the family income had to be declared. Harry was earning £138 a year as a tram driver and Eva, now teaching at a Hessle Road school, was earning £151, out of which she had to repay £31 a year on the loan she had taken out for her college course. Eventually, after an anxious wait, Dan heard that Hull University College had awarded him an adult scholarship of £50 a year for the next three years, an adequate amount if he continued to live at home. So in October 1934, shortly before his twenty-first birthday, he was all set to start on a degree course.

★★★

Photographs of Dan taken about this time show a fresh-faced, young man, with fine features and lots of curly hair (an asset enjoyed by all the Billanys), wearing an open-necked shirt and sports jacket, with a fountain pen in the top pocket. Holiday snaps show him in shorts beside his bike, with a backdrop of a ruined abbey, a lake, or a mountain scene; or cross-legged sitting in front of a tent wearing a black one-piece swimming costume with a singlet top. But he is always smiling, a wide open grin which gives a clear indication of his cheerful, friendly personality.

Leisure time was often spent with Reg Bloomfield, a contemporary of Dan's and Leo's at the Technical College. Reg's family had a six berth house-boat, the

ents went off alone to Whitby for a holiday in the summer of 1935; unlike their children, Harry and Elsie were of a generation that didn't take holidays. Dan and his sisters also visited the Lake District, which Dan loved, partly because of its association with the Lakeland poets; they went to Derbyshire and visited Derwent Hall, now under water, victim of a valley flooded to make a reservoir; they marvelled at Fountains Abbey, at Canterbury Cathedral and at the sights of London. In 1935 Dan and Reg cycled as far as North Wales, visiting all the beauty spots and reaching Holyhead. They climbed Snowdon in the mist and got soaked on several occasions but their postcards home continued to be full of high spirits. The following year they cycled in one day to Norwich where they stayed with Reg's uncle and his family. Throughout the thirties, they enjoyed many such holidays. Sunburnt, healthy and eating well, (Dan often described the meals he cooked in his postcards home), they covered large distances. Dan seemed to be completely cured of the asthma which had afflicted him as a child. He loved the escapist element of these trips; he was moved by the beauty of natural things and remoteness held a special appeal for him.

Throughout this carefree period, both Eva and Joan had many boyfriends. There was Joe, Eva's friend, of whom she was very fond, but rather ashamed because he was only a milkman. The romance did not last, but under Eva's influence Joe resumed studies at night class and eventually became a teacher. Joan had a boyfriend with a motor-bike and she would ride pillion with Bonzo sitting on the seat between them, perfectly relaxed and steady as a rock. But Dan had no time for girls; he still found himself intimidated and easily embarrassed in their company, so he avoided contact and concentrated on all the other interests that were crowding into his life.

As Dan's experiences had widened, so had his tastes. His love of classical music was an example of the way he was gravitating towards what he considered to be a more intellectual aspect of life and modifying his Hull accent was another part of this development. Good food, smart clothes and especially intelligent and stylish company delighted him; he took to them naturally, and tried to encourage the family to follow in his footsteps. He was often invited to dinner parties and drew inspiration from these to cook for his family innovative dishes which he presented with a flourish at the Lakeside Grove dining table. But they were less interested in his operatic records and after grudgingly listening to a selection, came down firmly on the side of Nelson Eddy and the melodic light music of the day. His mother was the most sympathetic and did her best to read the books Dan recommended, although it is doubtful if she made much of Ezra Pound's *Guide to Kulchur*. Dan continued to pursue his cosmopolitan tastes, but this did not distance him from his parents and sisters. He was gradually taking over the responsibility of the head of the family, and they looked up to him proudly, in awe of the transformation that was taking place.

1. Dan Eva and Joan. A studio portrait taken at J J Payne's on Anlaby Road when Dan was ten years old. This was at a time when the Billanys were going through a lot of problems, the father recovering from tuberculosis had just started regular work for the first time in years and the new baby was very ill and shortly to die. Nevertheless, family pride meant that the children were dressed in their best and with faces scrubbed clean, taken down to the photographers to record their images for the family album.

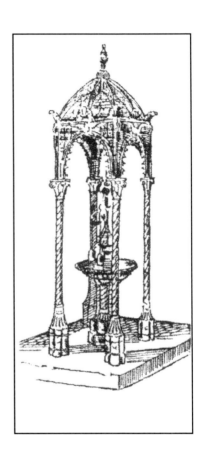

ONE PENNY.

MARK HASTINGS'
(Guy Hayley)
RADICAL SONGS

FOR

WORKING MEN.

SPECIALLY COMPOSED

FOR

ELECTION MEETINGS

IN SUPPORT OF

MR. N. B. BILLANY.

HULL, MAY, 1885.

To be had Wholesale or Retail of
E. WING & SON, STATIONERS, 7, GEORGE-ST.

MICHAEL WALLER, PRINTER, LOWGATE, HULL.

2. Neiles Boynton Billany (1826-1896). Dan's great-grandfather was a champion of Hull's working men and the first weekly-waged man to stand for Parliament. Pictured with him is a sketch of the drinking fountain erected in West Park to honour his memory, and the cover of Mark Hastings' Radical Songs specially composed for his election campaign. *(Picture by Turner & Drinkwater)*

3a. Dan's grandparents Lincoln Billany and his wife Betsy. He was involved in Union politics all his life, even travelling to the USA in his role as District Secretary to the Boilermakers' Society. But he was a difficult, moody man, shamefully neglecting his wife who once her children had grown up, divorced him. *(Pictures by The Seaman Studio)*

3b. Louisa Wilson, Dan's maternal grandmother pictured here with her second husband Arthur Thackeray. Dan described her as "an angel" because she was a constant support to his family in the early days when they were struggling against poverty and ill-health.

4a. Elsie and Harry, Dan's parents, on a rare day out at the seaside in the carefree days before their marriage. The pose is typical, Harry swankily nonchalant and brimming with confidence, Elsie reticent but nonetheless smiling broadly under her huge hat. You can see she adores him.

4b. A more serious picture of Harry taken some years later with his brother, both in their First World War uniforms. Harry on the right was serving with the Royal Navy, Mick on the left with the army. Both were lucky enough to come through the action unscathed.

5a. The Eureka Cinema on Hessle Road not far from the top of Devon Street. This was the Billanys' local picture palace which they all attended regularly throughout the 20s and 30s when it was a fine building with an ornate. white marble facade. This picture taken in 1992 shows it in a sadly dilapidated state. *(Picture by Barry Thompson)*

5b. Dan's first job at age 14 was that of an errand boy at Frank Plummer's High Class Fruit Shop. These snaps show him as a cheeky young lad smiling both in sunshine and rain. Despite problems with bronchitis which meant a real struggle delivering heavy loads, he persevered for over a year before moving on to an electrical apprenticeship.

6. Auntie Beattie in an elegant pose. She was the manageress of Frank Plummer's shop and well-off enough to splash out on fashionable clothes, such as this elaborately embroidered gown. She often handed down garments she had tired of to her younger sister Elsie, who is seen below wearing the same dress in a carefully arranged family portrait. Even Harry has dressed up for the occasion this time. *(Pictures by J J Payne)*

7. Two typical snaps of Dan during his student years taken with Joan's box camera. The photograph above shows him reading on the couch at Lakeside Grove. The photograph below, in lighter mood, is taken in the garden with Bonzo. Observe the width of his plus fours.

8a. Private Billany of B Company, Royal Army Service Corps, shortly after he enlisted in 1940. His newly shorn hair and cap at a jaunty angle make him look younger than his 25 years.

8b. Second Lieutenant Billany of' The East Yorkshire Regiment. He obtained his commission in July 1941 and posed for the usual portrait. Once again he is doing his best to look the part.

8c. While Dan was engaged in officer training he was recalled to Hull when the house in Lakeside Grove was demolished during the bombing of Spring 1941. This picture shows a typical scene of Hull homes destroyed by enemy action, the terrible aftermath of a Luftwaffe attack. (*Taken from "A North East Coast Town" by T. Geraghty*)

Chapter 8
A season of calm weather

The University of Hull at which Dan enrolled in October 1934 was a very different place from the one that exists on the same site today. In fact it wasn't a university at all, simply a college, an outpost of London University, which prescribed the curriculum, set the exams and awarded the degrees. The College had been founded seven years earlier, after lengthy financial negotiations, discussions and wrangling which ended in 1922 when T R Ferens, the local industrialist and philanthropist, bought the original three-field site on the northern outskirts of the city. Soon afterwards he gave a quarter of a million pounds, a colossal sum in those days, but even with such an endowment the early years were financially precarious.

Two brick buildings, separated by a sunken grassed area known as 'the soup-plate', were all that existed when the college opened in October 1928. There were only sixteen staff and thirty-nine students! The venture flourished and expanded during the next six years and when Dan arrived there were 199 students. Over half of them were living in Halls of Residence at Cottingham, the men in Needler Hall, and the women, who were outnumbered four to one, in Thwaite Hall. Dan lived at Lakeside Grove with his parents and cycled across the city each day. There were only three staff in the English Department and fewer than twenty students in his year. This was a far cry from 'the dreaming spires', but it did mean that local young people of limited means could have a university education, impossible for those who could not afford the expense of living away from home in Leeds, Manchester or even further afield.

The social life of the College's handful of students was handicapped by their lack of numbers. It was rather like a party where there are not enough guests to make it go with a swing. Nevertheless, there were some outstanding personalities around, who worked hard for their community and before long the Students Union was established, sports teams were set up and enrolled in local leagues, and various societies were started. But most were poorly attended and their committees had a struggle to keep them going. Dan for a while was the secretary of The Socialist Group, but it folded in 1936. Even dances, held in the College or the Halls, were poorly attended; the men in general were reluctant to participate and the girls were often left to gossip on the sidelines. Dan avoided such occasions, as he did the sporting activities.

Dan's finances were by no means straight-forward. After a protracted struggle, involving endless forms and means tests, he had secured a College scholarship of £50 a year, which after the deduction of tuition fees and other expenses, left him with £8 9s 4d a term, not a great deal to live on, so he applied for an extra grant from the Hull Education Committee. They declined, aware that Dan was also applying for a continuation of the Riley-Luxton scholarship which he had been given during his period of private study in 1933-4. Dan pressed for news of the Riley-Luxton, but was kept waiting for a decision until October 1934, and in the end was refused. He appealed to Hull Education Committee again and was awarded an extra £50 per year, but it was November before the money came through.

Both grants were dependent on his satisfactory progress in his main course, English, and subsidiaries, French, Latin and Economics. By November he was already in trouble when his French professor reported to the Registrar "while his work with me is *fairly satisfactory*, the same cannot be said of his written work with my assistant to whom he has given only two exercises out of a possible four. *No* excuse was supplied in both cases." Professor MacInnes continued drily that he would draw Dan's attention to the matter with a timely warning. This may better be described as the ultimate threat: Work or your money's in danger! Spring term came and there was not much improvement. Dan received another warning, this time for the low marks he scored in English; he must re-sit the examination. Not a very promising start, especially for a man who had been called a "marvel". The following year there was more criticism. Dan passed his referred English examination but after Christmas was in trouble again. One of his tutors complained of his slackness, for which she could find no excuse and gave her opinion that he was "distinctly undisciplined". Again the college threatened to discontinue his grant unless there was an improvement.

It seems that having reached his goal of gaining entry to the university, Dan was thoroughly disappointed by the regime that he found there. He was used to working on his own at a level far higher than the simple translation exercises he was being set. The three years he spent as an undergraduate are somewhat of a mystery. He never used that period of his life in his writing and he seldom mentioned his tutors or the material he was studying in letters or conversation. Probably he found it all so dull that he just got on with more interesting things, taking his education into his own hands rather than going along with that on offer at Hull College. There is no doubt about his brilliance; some of his essays, on Literature and Economics, which survive from this period show a remarkable perception, and are written in a confident and often amusing style. For example, in considering Dickens' heroines he sums up their wishy-washiness in the phrase, "Little Nell, Little Dorritt and all the other little ninnies."

It was not long before Dan met Horace Mason, a fellow English student who was to become a close friend. Horace was a strong-minded and intelligent man who had definite ideas about higher education and voiced his criticism of the College and in particular the English department in no uncertain terms. Unlike most of his fellow students, whose aim was to conform, to please the lecturers and to get a good degree, he was keen to promote interaction between staff and students, discussion linking various elements of the curriculum, a breadth of education which was outside the examination syllabus. The Hull College with its small tightly-knit departments, its Cercle Francais, its Scientific Soc. was unable to provide this and its students were apathetic to Horace's exhortations. He was a founder of The Art and Life Society, but it failed due to lack of interest; he organised play readings at the Dramatic Society of obscure and thought-provoking plays; he and a small group of supporters formed The Passing Dogs Club, a literary society affiliated to the Scrutiny movement, but no more was heard of it after 1934. Dan inevitably gravitated towards this interesting character, and many of his views on education were influenced by Horace Mason.

Both men were in their twenties, living locally with their parents and therefore separated from the social life associated with the Halls of Residence. This and their more mature attitude perhaps explain why they did not mix with the general run of students. Dan is remembered only vaguely by contemporaries as a rather awesome figure. He was an articulate conversationalist who, if he could be enticed into discussion, would display a biting wit and mordant sense of humour. But although his voice was occasionally heard in the Library and the Men's Common Room, raised in earnest argument, generally he preferred to hold himself aloof.

The Torch was the student magazine, run by a small group of devotees, most of them from the English Department. It was a well-produced magazine, financed partly by the College and partly by local advertising, issued three times a year. It contained a mixture of reports of College activities, original pieces of writing, letters and comment. In 1935, when Horace Mason took over the role of editor, his first task was to persuade people to write for *The Torch*. This seemed an ideal outlet for Dan's literary ambitions and he willingly offered material for publication. From then on, he regularly contributed poetry, short stories, critical articles, book reviews, and later he served on the committee and helped to write the editorials.

Dan was in accord with Horace Mason's views on education. He maintained that the duty of the university teacher is to educate the whole man - to broaden his understanding with as wide a range of experiences as possible - to encourage him to read, think, and decide for himself; just the opposite of the spoon-feeding on which most of the college students relied. Horace and Dan both set about educating themselves outside the curriculum. Their breadth of reading was phenomenal. No wonder Dan failed to hand in his French translations or to mug up for an Anglo-Saxon test; he felt he had much better things to do with his time. And away from the university there were many other demands, politics of course, and classical music, to which he introduced Horace. Both men were involved with The Fellowship of Debate, a left wing group which flourished in the town during the 1930s. In the Autumn Session of 1937, Horace Mason organised the Book Circle and Dan delivered a lecture on *The Platonic Spirit in English Poetry*.

At the same time Dan was engaged on his first novel and experimenting with poetry. It was incredibly varied: satirical verses in rhyming couplets after the style of Pope; experimental poems using complicated rhyme patterns and metres; poems with obscure classical references; love poetry; political comment; sentimental songs; esoteric jokes. In *Sonnet of Sacco and Vanzetti*, written in 1938, Dan's interest in classical music combines with his political convictions in referring back to the famous case of the 1920s, which Dan's father had so forcefully brought to the attention of his children.

SONNET OF SACCO AND VANZETTI
A record of Caruso

You slid the needle on, and there began
   The singing of Caruso: and to you
   It seemed the free-voiced singer also knew
The strength and capability of man.

Since then, you have been silenced, and the voice
   Sings to a world that could not well admit
   Such splendour, with the power to menace it
And finds its strength barbarity and noise.

But yon black night sings morning to our ears,
   Your voice is silence and your silence sings,
   The nightingale, Caruso, keeps his wings -
Your blended voices singing through your tears,
   High over Murder's crafty head are hurled;
   The Internationale thunders round the world.

It is a moving, beautifully written poem, in which he compares the singing of Caruso with the soaring spirits of Sacco and Vanzetti, so cruelly silenced. They were two Italian immigrants who had been framed, convicted of murder and executed, at the height of America's 'Red Scare'. Dan would have been delighted to know that in August 1997, seventy years after their deaths, the mayor of Boston finally exonerated them by dedicating a memorial to their memory in the city where they were condemned.

Dan liked to be controversial. The 1938 editorial committee of *The Torch* (which no longer included Horace) was reluctant to publish his poem called *Thank You, Miss Bottomly!*, in which an infant school headmistress is exhorting her pupils to say the Lord's Prayer *nicely*. Eventually on the third or fourth attempt the children get it completely right, and the hall roof opens.

Dan Billany ~

"The Magic Door"

"Dan Billany – Hull's Lost
Hero" ~ Valerie Reeves &
Valerie Showan.

But just as they finished, a wondrous light
Which blazed through the hall showed a startling sight,
For over Miss Bottomly, like a spell,
The sky sprang apart and the roof as well,
And the voice of the Lord - you could hear each letter -
Said "Thank you Miss Bottomly! That was better."
Miss Bottomly smiled distinctly twice,
And said, "Isn't that nice children? Isn't that nice?
I'm sure if tomorrow's a very nice day,
We shall give all you children an extra long play."

The committee agreed to publish it in the end, but anonymously. There was a large Education Faculty at the college and the students studying teaching theory, or engaged in teaching practice, were among those who thoroughly enjoyed the joke.

★★★

Dan's first novel, *A Season of Calm Weather*, was written in the front room of his parents' house at Lakeside Grove about this time, probably during 1936 or 1937. The title is taken from Wordsworth's *Intimations of Immortality*, and the main theme is a celebration of childhood.

It is a love story centred round the passion that Philip, a young teacher, develops for a twelve year old boy. There are two strands to the novel, the political and the sexual, which are only loosely connected and this is a weakness. The account of Philip's flirtation with communism and his friendship with Felix La Roche has already been discussed in the previous chapter as this much is autobiographical.

But the other element, the love story, is fantasy, a daring subject presented without any ambiguity or excuses. The moment Philip sees Dickie Bryant, he falls in love with him.

The first symptom which he experienced was a sort of catch of the breath, which extended right through him, in involuntary homage to the surprise of sudden beauty - in a way the sort of astonished awe which one feels when a lovely musical phrase floats in above the rhythm of the violins in a Beethoven symphony. Love always begins with this divine shock.

And as the relationship progresses, so does the intensity of his feelings. He wants to touch him, to put his arms round him, to kiss him; he tries to convince himself that his motives are purely honourable, that his love is protective and compassionate, but at the same time he is fully aware that it could be misinterpreted. Inevitably this is what happens. Dickie's school friends start sniggering, the headmaster becomes alarmed and informs the parents. They are incensed and forbid their son to see Philip again. But by now he is so passionately involved that he cannot keep away from the boy, even when the police are informed and warn him off in the strongest of terms.

It is a full length novel, carefully structured and fluently expressed which must have taken the best part of a year to write. Dan was obviously satisfied with it as he sent the manuscript to several publishers towards the end of 1937. They all rejected it but it is worth consideration for what it indicates about Dan's state of mind at the time. He often said about himself that he was still a child, that he didn't feel grown up in comparison with his friends. He seemed to be avoiding adult relationships with women, whom he found physically unappealing. Instead he turned to children, in particular boys. He enjoyed their company, wanted to instruct and help them in a friendly, caring manner, as an equal rather than in the heavy-handed traditional role of the school-master or Victorian father. Did he also find children sexually attractive, as Philip did? He certainly seems to identify very strongly with Philip's feelings, while at the same time being aware of the terrible pitfalls surrounding such a passion.

A Season of Calm Weather is written in the third person but told entirely from the point of view of Philip, who shares a flat with his friend Len. Both teach at the Girls' High School, but their house overlooks a boys' elementary school, and it is in the playground there that Philip first sees and falls in love with Dickie. He is introduced into the flat when he throws a cricket ball through their open window, and after that Philip invites him up on a whole string of excuses, to play the piano, to get help with his homework, to come for tea. Dickie is presented as a typical boy, who uses slang expressions, and is interested in guns, comics, and stink bombs. Philip goes along with this, he seems to enjoy boyish activities himself and, like Dan, says on more than one occasion that he doesn't feel grown up. However it is not long before he puts his arm round the boy, and eventually kisses him; Dickie reluctantly tolerates this because he enjoys Philip's company.

Dickie's parents are pleased that their son has got a friend who is a teacher, a cut above the average, and they suggest that he should spend a summer holiday with them at Sedgeley (a thinly disguised Leven) where they have a house boat. These three weeks are the high spot of the story. In the previous chapter we have quoted Dan's description of the scene on the canal as dusk falls. The romantic mood continues - fish and chip suppers together on the sofa in the bungalow Philip has rented, and when the weather breaks, a scene when Dickie gets wet through and Philip dries him off, and wraps him in a blanket in front of the fire.

Philip's flat-mate Len, in contrast, is getting on with heterosexual activities and by the summer has formed a serious relationship with Monica, the house-maid. Before long they are preparing to marry and move to the south of England, where Len has been offered a headship. Len is very concerned about the predicament that Philip finds himself in, particularly when the bubble bursts, Dickie's parents turn nasty and the police are brought in. He does his best to help and advise his friend, but Philip is so besotted that he descends into utter misery, losing interest in everything except his overwhelming desire to see Dickie again.

It is at this stage that Len finds in the bureau drawer several sheets of notes that Philip has written. They begin with a dissertation on King Lear's love for the Fool, and more generally, boys as love objects in Shakespeare's plays. This broadens into an essay on the historical precedent for, and justification of, adult men's love for boys. It is a well researched piece with lots of quotations and references, encompassing the whole range of literature, from Plato to the present time.

In contrast with this reasoned argument, Philip's notes also include rough drafts of several poems, which present his emotional response to the situation.

> I tremble at your footsteps, Child;
>   Oh, do not grieve me!
> Let your government be mild
>   And never leave me.
> You that are a living light,
> Bud and flower in my sight,
> Sun and lily ever white.
>
> I would have so much to hide
>   Should you deceive me;
> Such a secret must be spied,
>   So never leave me;
> Empty Nothing could not sprout
> Feathers fine enough to flout,
> So the truth would soon come out.
>
> Naturally you must play,
>   But never leave me;
> Dear, I have no other day,
>   Oh never leave me;
> Although angels filled the skies,
> Still for me the whole world lies
> Darkness, child, without your eyes.

The main thrust of the poem is "Oh never leave me", but inevitably this is what must happen to a man who falls in love with a child. For he will grow up, will change into another person, and vanish. And this is how the novel ends. The police charges are dropped, Philip spends the Christmas holiday in despair

capable, a relaxed young man who knew where he was going, a well-adjusted, happy fellow who was just a bit shy with girls.

In spite of earlier hiccups, Dan passed his retakes, satisfied his tutors, safeguarded his grant, and in June 1937 was awarded an Honours English degree, grade 2.1. He was not disappointed to have missed a First; in his view the paper qualification was the least important thing about his education. In a letter to Leo Peters, his political friend who by this time had left Hull, he wrote, on July 31st 1937,

> If you take my advice, you won't put yourself to any trouble collecting letters to put after your name; it doesn't make me feel the least bit taller, and its commercial value appears to be nil; I'm going to be on the dole if I don't look out. What a wash-out a degree is; academic laurels certainly aren't evergreen. Still I've had £300 out of it, so I shouldn't grumble. But dear me! Ah for a nice quiet country oasis, a farmhouse or a pub, where I could stop being an undergrad, or a grad, or a literary bloke, and start being alive. Believe me, I never worked hard at College, but all the same the deadly mental stricture of the place soaked into me, if a stricture can soak, and gave me a perpetual subconscious headache which I haven't shaken off yet.

And in the last paragraph of the letter, he enquires,

> Have you propagated your species yet? It's a question which intrigues me, because, as one who has chosen to spend his life romping on the nursery carpets, I am amazed and thrilled by those of my playmates - such as you - who grow up, and join the grave, important people who occasionally peep in at me through the window and smile. You see what I mean; a son of yours would be, a priori, rather wonderful.

Why was Dan so reluctant to grow up? Was it linked to his confusion about his sexuality, an unwillingness to face the problem and so to take refuge in childhood? Partly, but there is more to it than that. Throughout his life Dan was fascinated by the idea of childhood, his own and others. And in all his novels there is at least one boy in a central role; in *The Magic Door* there are thirty of them. He railed often about the iniquities visited on children by adults, and, although an atheist, frequently quoted Christ's words "Suffer little children to come unto me..." In his writing, and in his life, Dan showed great compassion for children, a sympathy and understanding unusual at that time. He would have loved to have had a son of his own; instead he had many substitute children. He deplored the idea of punishing a child and the rigid discipline of school life was anathema to him. In this respect he was well ahead of his time.

A large proportion of the college students, including Dan, stayed on for a Teacher Training year after graduation, often with a feeling of resentment. It was muttered in some quarters that Hull College was just churning out fodder for the elementary schools. There was a surfeit of teachers at this time, and to land a post in a secondary school where the teaching was academic and geared towards examinations, was exceptional. The elementary schools were single sex establishments and took pupils from the age of five to fourteen, with no particular objective beyond a general grounding in the three R's. But this suited Dan as he was enthusiastic to put into practice his and Horace's theories about freedom in education. Horace had by this time joined the staff of the University Library, but after the war he too became a teacher, working with African children in remote parts of Kenya and Tanzania.

The elusive Riley-Luxton Foundation awarded Dan £50 for his Teacher Training year, and under the guidance of his tutor, R K Robertson, he completed teaching practice and passed his exams, in spite of a most unorthodox approach. In June 1938 he became a qualified teacher and was appointed by the local Education Committee to "a Hull school" at a salary of £204 a year, although at this time it was not specified which school that would be.

Chapter 9

A most unusual teacher

D an Billany joined the staff of Chiltern Street School in September 1938. There was an air of expectation among the boys of Standard Three that morning. Word had got around that this was no ordinary teacher and from the moment the headmaster brought him in, they knew that this man was special. He surprised them immediately when he introduced himself.

"I don't expect you to call me Mr Billany," he said. "My name is Dan."

He was as different from the normal run of school teachers as any boy could hope for and it didn't take long for him and his class to shake down into an easy-going and comfortable relationship. They all called him Dan, and soon it was accepted and seemed perfectly natural, except in front of Mr Stebbings, the headmaster. These boys, thirty-one of them aged nine and ten years, were rough kids from a poor part of Hull, and this was a time when money was short everywhere. Poor housing, inadequate food and clothing were common, but by contrast, school was an exciting, even magical world if you were in Dan's class.

Unlike every other teacher they had encountered, this one didn't wield his authority over them; he didn't have a cane; he didn't use sarcasm, or order them about, or tell them they were wrong. In other classrooms discipline was harsh. Inattention was rewarded by a flying piece of chalk or board-rubber, the cane was in frequent use, and pupils were expected to sit still and in silence. But Dan had a totally different approach. Neighbouring classes were amazed by the noise that emanated from his room, the pupils envious of the laughter that they heard, the teachers frowning with disapproval.

Dan's ability to tell stories and to make lessons interesting transformed life at school for his class of boys. History lessons were a good example. They always started in the same way with Dan drawing an elaborate arched doorway on the blackboard.

"Right now, who's going to knock on the door today?"

Eager hands went up all round the classroom. "Me, Dan, me, me, me!" A boy was chosen to knock, and the story began. The whole class were mesmerised as Dan led them in imagination through the door, back into time where they encountered numerous characters from history, talked with them, joked with them and joined in their adventures. They visited Julius Caesar, and fought in a battle with Ancient Britons; one day they found themselves in Rome at the slave market where they met Pope Gregory, who looked at them closely and uttered those famous words, "Not Angles but Angels."

We can share in these lessons, because later Dan wove them into a children's adventure story, a fast moving tale full of excitement and schoolboy humour. He called it *The Magic Door*. It is the story of a class of thirty-one boys, and their teacher, Mr Rocket. One morning, a boy called Bartlett arrives at school with a strange, triangular piece of metal he has found. When the boys press Mr Rocket to identify it, he is nonplussed but to cover his ignorance offers the suggestion that it could be a Chinese teapot stand. This is ridiculed, and much speculation and argument ensues until Bartlett points out that it may be a door-knocker.

"What a foolish door-knocker that would be," said Mr Rocket, with a gentle smile. "You mean - hold it up like that," he held up the little piece of metal, "and then bang with it - so." He banged with it as he spoke, and then an amazing thing happened; as he moved the piece of metal twice forward, from empty air came two tremendous knocks, just as if he had knocked on an iron door. When Mr Rocket looked round he saw an amazing sight. There, standing in the wall of the room and cutting through the middle of the blackboard, ... was a splendid door, made of shining green metal, with black metal scrollwork on it, and a decorated archway around it, with precious stones flashing in the pattern of the decoration ... And with a grinding, creaking, squeaking, metallic noise from its enormous hinges the great door was swinging open.

While the boys are all hiding under their desks in terror, Mr Rocket, who has nerves of steel, backs out from the cupboard he has squeezed into, steps forward into the strange light emanating from behind the door, and faces the figure of a Winged Boy, wearing gold sandals, who cries, "What is your will?"

Mr Rocket could not think of anything to say; and after glancing doubtfully at his watch, he said: "Can you tell me the right time?"
"It's always the right time," said the boy.

And so begins a series of visits back in time, sometimes with Mr Rocket, sometimes without him. His nerves of steel come in very useful in the more hair-raising episodes. On their very first visit they are mauled by wolves in a primeval forest; another time they meet the druids who attempt to sacrifice Gordon Merritt by roasting him alive on the altar fire at Stonehenge. Being sold as slaves is pretty scary too, but all the adventures are tremendous fun, and often extremely funny as well.

Take for example their visit to Julius Caesar. They try to put him right about British History, quoting Mr Rocket, (on this occasion safely back in the classroom) as their authority. Caesar is quite impressed until they tell him that Brutus and Cassius are going to murder him, at which point he dismisses them as lunatics.

However the most interesting characters are not the historical ones but the boys and their teacher. This is how they are introduced in the first paragraph of the book

Perhaps they were the noisiest set of boys you ever saw; or perhaps not, but they got more opportunity. Finally, Mr Rocket had what seemed a bright idea. It was a bright idea for him. He told them to write a diary each morning, as soon as they came into the school. "What's a diary?" they wanted to know, and Mr Rocket said it was a book where you put all you did each day, so that when you grew up you would be able to see what you had done when you were young. Standard Three said they didn't want to know what they did when they were young when they grew up; so Mr Rocket said "Never you mind about that, you write a diary, and do as you're told." So that became the regular thing, and Standard Three were not quite so noisy for the first two minutes each day.

They are of course his class at Chiltern Street - lively, answering back, joking. One of them recently read *The Magic Door* for the first time. He said that the book gives a true feeling of what life was like in Dan's class; and that most of the pupils were role models for Huckleberry Finn. He told us that they did keep a daily diary and he identified a number of the boys in the story with his fellow pupils.

Like so much of Dan's writing, *The Magic Door* is successful because it is real. In the original manuscript, the teacher is called Mr Billany and the boys bear the names of the thirty-one pupils in his class. The publisher, Thomas Nelson, insisted that the names were changed, in case of legal action, so fictitious ones were substituted. Dan took a long time to find a suitable name for the teacher, before hitting on Mr Rocket, which fitted the character perfectly. (Was he influenced by the fact that the Sheriff of Hull at the time was a Mr W Rockett?) But there was one name which wasn't changed. That was Jack Crossley. He was a clever, lively lad who had attracted Dan's attention from the start by his cheeky good humour. He had left Hull sometime during the year when his family moved to Leeds. Naturally he was upset at having to leave such an exciting class and so Dan corresponded with him and kept him in touch with their adventures. When the book came to be published, it was dedicated to him. His parents had to give written permission for this and for Jack's real name to be used.

★★★

It would seem that Dan's unusual educational methods were working. But he was not without detractors. Mr Stebbings, the headmaster, was very dubious about his approach; Dan didn't argue; he just smiled and carried on. And the other staff were not sympathetic. They felt he was undermining authority in the school, which of course he was; this was his intention. His boys were undoubtedly very noisy and unruly. They were allowed to answer back, to argue, to question opinions, but Dan's methods did work in this context. The class was taught as a group by Dan for nearly all subjects, so within that unit the boundaries were set and the pupil-teacher relationship established.

During his Teacher Training year, Dan had read widely, visited schools, talked with teachers of all persuasions, and come to the conclusion that there had to be a better way of educating children than the current one. The harshness of his own schooldays still rankled with him.

Not one educator, from Plato to Herbart, has started by looking at a child. That's where education begins, with the child, not with any ideological schemes we may have about existence. Educators have worked backwards, in trying to fit the child to their ideas. They shouldn't have any ideas, to begin with; they should start from the child, which is not an idea, but a fact. Children should be allowed to develop to the full the powers which are growing within them; never mind whether these powers are at variance with the present state of the world; have confidence in the child, and let it grow. If society then fails to fit the child, so much the worse for society; education has done too much of this squaring of round pegs to get them into square holes; let the holes be altered now.

It sounds a fairly reasonable argument to modern ears, but at the time it was revolutionary. This quotation comes from *Paul*, another unpublished work, which is an attempt to understand children, their problems, fears, hopes and relationships, both with each other and with adults. It tells the story of Paul (Dan himself thinly disguised), a student on teaching practice who disagrees with authoritarian ideas and is eager to put his own theories to the test. He recalls his own schooldays and the harsh treatment he and his classmates suffered at the hands of characters like Old Lewis. In contrast, Paul is determined to treat his pupils with sympathy and understanding.

Firstly he presents the traditional viewpoint in the person of the headmaster who advises, "Above all, you must remain outside the class, and above them if you see what I mean. The teacher must have dignity or the class won't look up to him ... you may find it as well to insist on absolutely military discipline for the first week or two ... " and the metal-work master who tells him, "... a teacher has the dignity of his profession to support. You can't be familiar with boys; they'll be all over you." On the subject of punishment, an experienced teacher tells him, "The cane is an essential part of the school; it's just as necessary for the boy's sake as for the teacher's." And, "The child is human ... you have to punish him to teach him the difference between wrong and right. Properly used, punishment is itself education."

However, Paul holds out against all this and maintains his position. He says, "I'm not arguing for lines as against corporal punishment; I'm arguing against all punishment." And, "I think unreasoning obedience is the last thing a teacher should demand. We're training human beings not automatons.." And, "I think it's possible to teach on quite a different basis. If you're always a friend to the kids, they'll never take advantage of you." Paul's education tutor, (possibly modelled on Dan's own tutor, R K Robertson), admits that privately he agrees with him but is worried that in practice, he will not be able to assert his authority.

However, Paul is undaunted and insists on teaching according to his theories. And it works; the children are interested, responsive and seem to be learning.

One of the biggest influences on Dan was the success of Summerhill, the experimental and controversial boarding school founded in 1921 by A S Neill and still in existence today. Dan had read Neill's book, *That Dreadful School*, published in 1937, and was immediately interested. He visited the school in Suffolk during his summer holiday and straightway felt at home there. He was shown round by a seven year old girl who had hurt her foot, so he carried her on his shoulders. She introduced him to staff, including A S Neill, and to the pupils. He spent a full day there, observing and talking; it is described in *Paul*. In Corky's chemistry class, an impatient twelve year old says to him, "Buck up Corky, let's get something written." The woman taking the infants' maths class is referred to as Jonesy. She ticks the sums they have got correct; the others she leaves unmarked for the pupils to try again. One little girl arrives late, just as the class is finishing; she pleads for a lesson, just a little one, so Jonesy gives in and agrees to give her ten minutes. Dan takes tea with the staff, occasionally interrupted by children poking their heads in from the garden to shout a greeting. He talks about his future in elementary schools, but admits, "However good my intentions towards the children, I find that by familiarity I am growing to tolerate all the things which I know to be wrong. By associating with bad teachers, I find I grow like them." In the evening he walked out to the field where some of the children were camping, and he sat and chatted with them round their fire.

"Will you be here tomorrow again?" said a boy.

"No," said Paul, "I'm going home tomorrow." He smiled and said with mock tragedy, "We will never see each other again."

Dan gained his Teaching Certificate in 1938. Professor A Victor Murray summed up his teaching practice in this testimonial,

He has little belief in orthodox methods of discipline and he treats his boys with a frankness and good humour which win their attention. He has also his own views about the content of teaching as well as its form, but while I doubt if he would ever get boys through an external examination he will make school life interesting and memorable for them.

So when he started his first job, he felt confident in his teaching style and determined to stick by his principles.

★★★

Chiltern Street School was a red brick Victorian building, opened by the Hull School Board in 1889. On one site were the Infants' School, the Boys' School and the Girls' School. It was ingeniously designed with brick walls separating the playgrounds, and different entrances in separate streets, so that the pupils should not be distracted from their studies by encounters with the opposite sex.

Nevertheless it was rumoured that some of the girls and one of the mistresses were quite keen to get a glimpse of handsome Mr Billany.

All subjects were taught by their class teacher in their own room. This was equipped with blackboard and wooden desks, each with a hole for the inkwell. They were arranged in pairs, with a back rest and tip up bench attached, uncomfortable to sit in, especially for boys with long legs, who were expected to sit still all day. Electricity had replaced the original gas lights, and there was a coal fired central heating system, the rooms near the boiler-house being the warmest; others were bitterly cold in the winter.

The playing field on Alliance Avenue was twenty minutes walk away, and in the summer the older pupils had an afternoon at Madeley Street swimming baths. But the main physical exercise was Drill, carried out in the playground. This entailed standing in rows, doing synchronised jerks of arms and legs to a pattern set by the teacher. This must have embodied all that Dan hated most in the restrictions of teaching at that time, the will to reduce the class to neat rows of automatons. So, for Standard Three, Drill went out and free games came in - impromptu football or cricket played against a wicket chalked on the playground wall.

Back in the classroom, English Literature, and particularly poetry played a large part in Standard Three's curriculum. Dan's method of teaching poetry was unusual. Instead of setting the boys to learn reams of stuff by heart, he encouraged them to talk about the poems, to ask themselves what were the poets' intentions, and to give their opinions and preferences. Favourites with them were such classics as *Lord Ullin's Daughter* and Rudyard Kipling's *If*. On the wall of their room hung a framed copy of *Vitai Lampada* by Henry Newbolt. It begins,

> There's a breathless hush in the Close tonight -
> Ten to make and the match to win -
> A bumping pitch and a blinding light,
> An hour to play and the last man in.
> And its not for the sake of a ribboned coat,
> Or the selfish hope of a season's fame,
> But his Captain's hand on his shoulder smote -
> "Play up! play up! and play the game!"

Each morning the whole class would recite this poem in unison. Its message of unselfishness, of working together for the good of the group appealed to the boys, who really did try to live up to its ideals. In fact they were a very close-knit group and this is clearly reflected in the team spirit shown by the class in *The Magic Door*.

On the same theme of "Play up! play up! and play the game!", Dan inspired his pupils with the true story of Private John Cunningham VC. He was a First World War hero, an old boy of Chiltern Street School, and there was an impressive commemorative plaque in the school hall celebrating his bravery. On 13th November 1916, the nineteen year old was one of an assault party attacking the enemy front line. In the confined space of the communication trench all the party except Cunningham were soon killed or wounded. But he advanced alone, lobbing grenades at the enemy, even going back to collect more ammunition. The sudden appearance of a party of ten Germans did not deter him; he killed them all and went on to clear the trench. For this he was awarded the Victoria Cross, the highest honour for gallantry. When he returned to Hull after his investiture, even though it was two o'clock in the morning, there was a band waiting to play for him at the station, and a large cheering crowd, who chaired him all the way back to his home in Edgar Street. This story of a local boy risen to hero status was a favourite with the class and Dan was often persuaded to retell it with all the action and drama brought vividly to life. In their hearts they longed for heroic adventures too.

For the rest of the school year, Dan's boys continued doing much as they liked, and most managed to learn and achieve something under his unorthodox regime. But as the summer holidays approached, it was clear that another war was imminent, and the lives of Standard Three and their teacher were going to be radically affected by it.

★★★

This poem by Dan Billany was published in *The Torch* magazine in June 1939.

TO JACK (AGE 10) WHO CRIED WHEN HE HAD
TO LEAVE ME AND GO TO LIVE IN LEEDS

"Cry no more my dear little child:
  Sorrow comes to old and young."
He dried his sweet blue eyes and smiled
  Long before the song was sung.

"Cry no more my dear little boy,
  You need not feel lonely, dear;
I won't let the miles destroy
  Love I learned when you were here.

"Cry no more, my dear little child.
  School will make us both feel sad.
I will see your school books piled
  Blankly on the desk you had.

"Cry no more, my almost son,
Cry no more, my sun, my star,
Times will find me, when you're gone,
Looking westward where you are.

"So cry no more, my sweet little child:
Partings old, but meetings young."
He dried his dear blue eyes and smiled
Long before the song was sung.

This sounds a strange poem to modern ears, very sugary and sentimental, in spite of the hint of self mockery in the last two lines. Sentimental it may be, but it was undoubtedly sincere. The Jack of the title is Jack Crossley, and the song Dan wrote for him was to comfort the boy who was desperately upset at having to leave his favourite teacher and move to a strange town. There may also have been other reasons for his unhappiness. We know that he was living with a step-father in Leeds, so possibly his mother's remarriage was all part of the upheaval. Dan addresses him as "my almost-son" and perhaps Jack saw in Dan a substitute father. Jack was a regular and lively correspondent. This is how he described his new teacher.

Mrs Muir (our teacher) didn't use to believe in caning kids before she came to our class and then she simply had to start. I don't like her so much. At first she once called me a dunce but when the exams came she said to me "Have you ever thought of going in for a scholarship Jack" so I said for a bit of fun because nobody in our class is frightened of her. I said "Do dunces go in for scholarships Miss?" and she looked at me aghast but didn't say nothing.

Leeds is not so far from Hull and they met quite often. In the holidays Jack would visit Dan and join him and his friends on cycle rides and camping trips. Jack's mother was happy to agree to this and so the friendship developed. But this was not so surprising. Dan felt a friendship for all his boys. He said on more than one occasion that he preferred their company to that of the staff, and he often joined them in the playground for a game during breaktime, rather than drinking tea in the staffroom. There is a Jack in *The Opera House Murders*, a ten year old, with a boyish sense of fun. And of course Jack Crossley himself, member of Standard Three, figures prominently in *The Magic Door*. This was not published until 1943, mainly because of delays caused by the war, and by that time Dan was abroad. But still he and Jack continued to correspond. Jack seems to have been an intelligent, lively boy; after school he became a reporter on the Leeds Evening Post and later a journalist, where he had the opportunity to review some of Dan's books.

Dan never strove to conceal his affection for his pupils and his pleasure in

69

their company. In the guise of Mr Rocket, he is as much one of the gang as any of the boys, apart from a few eccentric grown-up habits like setting them long division sums or suggesting they learn poems. But inevitably one has to ask the question, just what was Dan's relationship with Jack, one a twenty-five year old man, the other a ten year old boy? One cannot help but think about the fictional situation in Dan's first novel, written three years earlier, that of Philip and the schoolboy he fell in love with. Was Dan in love with Jack, did he have the same yearnings as Philip, the same admiration for the child's beauty and grace? Possibly there were such feelings, but they were never manifest. It was simply a warm, relaxed, absorbing friendship between two people who enjoyed each other's company. In the 1930s such a friendship was easily accepted without comment.

During his teaching practice, Dan had written in *Paul*,

> I've never quite got used to being grown up; I think I never will. When I stand behind the teacher's desk, I can't really feel that I've a right to be there; half of me, at least, is still sitting with the kids on the other side. How does one manage to grow up?

There was a dichotomy in Dan's self perception; he often said that he didn't feel grown up and he harks back to childhood recollections, to the transient quality of childhood, to Wordsworth's *Intimations of Immortality;* but at the same time he feels a strong responsibility to look after young people, to protect them from the harshnesses of life. The role of 'parent figure' was one which he willingly shouldered in relation to his own family; he was a sympathetic supporter of his little sister Joan and later a great source of strength to his parents. As a teacher, he was very concerned to help the disturbed, the under-achiever or the disadvantaged pupil. For example at Chiltern Street, he patiently attempted to coax out the boy who spent most of the day crouched under his desk, the one at whom other staff shouted, or aimed a passing blow. And he pestered the authorities about a child with very poor eyesight whose parents couldn't be bothered to take him to the clinic. Later in the army he was to be a father-figure to the young men in his platoon, while at the same time feeling very small and vulnerable himself.

Chapter 10

Into war and into print

Dan certainly took teaching very seriously and battled hard to prove that his unusual methods were workable, but he had not lost sight of his main ambition which was to be a writer. He always had some piece on the go - poetry, plays, articles and during his first year of teaching, evenings were spent at the typewriter on another big project, his third novel which is called *Living Amongst Boys*. Like the previous two, it is closely based on himself and his experiences, this time in the classroom. And the same theme, that of childhood and the exploitation of children by adults, dominates. By the summer of 1939 it was finished and Dan was sending it on the rounds of the publishers. Sadly they all turned it down and it has never been published, which is a pity because it is a remarkable story.

In *Living Amongst Boys* the main character is once again Paul Sanderson, now in his first teaching post, in charge of Standard Three at Westcar Boys' School. This part is modelled very closely on Dan's experiences at Chiltern Street, including the innovative history lessons conducted by way of the Magic Door. It is told with lovely humorous touches, as Paul battles to instigate his child-centred methods. When he arrives late, which is regularly, the class choruses, "Good morning dear teacher, good morning to you!" And during one particularly chaotic session, he says, "I gave orders in a sinister whisper looking like a snake at the boys."

Eventually Paul gives up and takes a post at a remote Welsh boarding school, where he is the only qualified member of staff, and the organisation is a shambles, rather like a cross between Dotheboys Hall and Llanabba Castle. The drunken headmaster takes great delight in both bathing and spanking the boys. Here Paul meets and is attracted by a housemaid called Ruby whom, he soon discovers, has been made pregnant by one of the boys. Paul saves the situation by marrying her but they cannot live together openly; she is packed off to her mother's while he continues to live in the school. Apart from Len Fewster's attempt to seduce a lady librarian in *A Season of Calm Weather*, this is the first time Dan describes a heterosexual affair, and it is cut short when Ruby is relegated to the background. The main sexual interest centres on the boys; Paul gets in deep trouble because he is willing to answer their questions about sex; and he becomes emotionally entangled with a twelve-year old called Alan who develops a crush on him. There is much humour in the story too, but drama and tragedy dominate and build up to a powerful climax in the last chapter.

Dan was still involved with the university magazine, *The Torch*; he served on the editorial committee for a while and continued to submit poems, short stories and book reviews. At least he was getting published somewhere, and in university circles his work was highly regarded.

Back at school after the summer holidays of 1939, everyone was preparing for evacuation, a complicated operation to move out of town huge numbers of school-children, mothers with babies, pregnant women, invalids and the disabled. They were sent to various East Yorkshire villages, or across the Humber into Lincolnshire. When the last bus load had left, Mr J D Heald, the co-ordinator for East Hull telephoned through to headquarters.

"What shall I do now?"

"Follow the buggers!" was the reply. So he did.

The Chiltern Street pupils were evacuated with their teachers to several small villages in the East Riding. The girls went to Hutton Cranswick, the boys to Nafferton or Kilham. The journey was by train, but the children had not been told where they were going. It was a real mystery trip, everyone in high spirits, some in a state of over-excitement. Each child carried a small haversack containing, among their other possessions, a gas mask and a postcard already stamped and addressed, ready to send home. The boys loved it although many of the mothers waving them off were in tears. The station loudspeakers, playing *The Teddy Bears' Picnic* added to the emotional atmosphere.

When they arrived at Driffield, the station was swarming with children from all round the area; one little boy who had wandered off on his own joined the wrong queue and was whisked off with a Roman Catholic School from Scarborough. He spent the whole war with them in a remote village, even though his mother had made special arrangements for him to be evacuated with his sister. The Chiltern Street boys were taken by bus to Nafferton, where at the Village Hall there was more noise and confusion as they were allocated to the local families. A number of the kids were crying by this time.

Enter Miss Barker, billeting officer, pushing her sit-up-and-beg bicycle. She linked a group of children together by a long piece of string tied round their wrists and set off down the village street, carrying a clip board with the list of names. As each child was found a billet she cut him free from the string and moved on. The remainder, still tethered in a line, trotted behind.

This is how Mrs Croft got her evacuee, a nine year old boy from Dan's class. She was leaning on the gate outside her farmhouse waiting for her husband coming back with the horse and cart. The crocodile of children approached. "Would you like an evacuee?" asked Miss Barker, but she refused, suspicious of town children, they none of them looked too clean. Eventually there were only a girl and boy left, and at the final house the woman chose the girl. This left Leslie Love, the last one without a home. On the way back through the village there was Mrs Croft still leaning on the gate. "Are you sure you don't want one?" said Miss Barker wearily. "Well I suppose he looks quite a strong lad, aye leave him here." And there he stayed for the next three years, and Mrs Croft became a second mother to him. She was a strict woman and he was set to work on the farm that very afternoon, and every other day too, but he was fed like he had never been fed before and was quickly assimilated into village life.

Back at the Village Hall, there remained eight small boys. They were feeling very dejected, the left-overs that nobody wanted, but a surprise was in store. Before long Dan Billany took charge of them and they were bundled into a van and driven about four miles to Pockthorpe Hall, an imposing three storied house, its stuccoed walls painted white and its curved drive leading up to a front door framed by ornately decorated pillars and surmounted by a large fanlight. The newcomers were driven round to the back entrance, alongside a brick wall, past the pig-sty, the stables and outbuildings and all the trappings of a working farm. There was a huge horse-chestnut tree beside the house, and the tired boys sat down there, relieved to have arrived at last. In its shade, on that baking hot afternoon, they wrote their postcards home.

Pockthorpe Hall was at the centre of a 700 acre farm. Behind it was the stable block, housing over fifty working horses, with its own blacksmith's forge nearby. Water was pumped from a deep well by a steam engine and piped over large distances to the rest of the farm. The boys were warned to keep out of the way of the farming activities, but their curiosity led them to investigate as much as they could; for example the Gamekeeper's Gallows of dead rats and crows hanging around the walls of the pig-sty was a source of great fascination. Dan, who lived with them at the Hall, had the job of supervising their leisure time and their education.

★★★

Pupils and teachers spent the next few weeks settling in and coming to terms with a totally new environment. Most had never even heard of Nafferton and many had not left Hull before. As the excitement wore off, many were homesick, missing their families and city life, some scared by their strange new surroundings. Even the quiet village street itself was dark and threatening in the blackout, quite different from the familiar closeness of their homes in Hull. Lots of children had never before seen a goat, a sheep or a cow, although horses were a common enough sight in the city. Geese were especially daunting, greeting anyone who tried to approach their territory with a frightening show of aggression. But there were compensations. One was the excellent food, and as much milk as you could drink, although most evacuees were expected to pull their weight, helping out on the farms and small-holdings, just like the village kids.

One memorable occasion was that of the Evacuation Concert in the Village Hall. A mixture of village and city children were delighted by the show put on by the teachers and anyone else who would volunteer. Dan's contribution was a Shadow Show; using a makeshift white screen, lit from behind by a lamp, he made a fantastic display of shadow shapes to accompany the story he told. The children, sitting cross-legged on the floor, hooted and cheered, and the story finished with everyone singing *Run, Rabbit, Run* at the tops of their voices.

For the boys who were billeted at Pockthorpe Hall, there was the added dimension of glorious, almost uninterrupted freedom. School had never been so free, and with Dan in charge of them, there was no pressure to conform. This was the closest Dan would come to the ideals of Summerhill. With only eight pupils, no timetable, no school-room even, there were unlimited opportunities for unstructured learning. One is reminded of his conversation at Summerhill with the boy who couldn't believe that at Dan's school there were thirty pupils in a class, and they sat in rows and did as they were told. When Dan said good-bye to him, and with mock tragedy, "We'll never see each other again," he was thinking that he would never have the chance to teach under such conditions, but here, for a few weeks, he had just that.

Autumn 1939 was exceptionally warm and sunny, and the war seemed very remote. In the isolation of Pockthorpe, Dan and the eight lads were able to enjoy adventures with few lessons to distract them. There was plenty of scope for the Huckleberry Finn element in the boys to develop, climbing trees, running wild in the countryside, playing on the farm. They had a marvellous time; it must have been like being on a never-ending camping trip. Their beds were straw mattresses on the boards of a large ground floor room. One night a swallow flew in through the open window and there was a mad scramble to catch it, which failed, when the bird found its own way out. Their weekly bath was taken, one after another, in a hip bath in the dairy under the supervision of one of the house-maids. There were plenty of new-laid eggs to eat and fresh milk to drink instead of the cups of sweet tea which they had been used to at home.

The rest of their class-mates were four miles away in Nafferton, attending the village school, but this was considered too far for the Pockthorpe boys to walk. Most of the time was spent out of doors including what passed for lessons. Dan would get them all to sit in a circle and they would begin with a task such as mental arithmetic. But it didn't last long and soon they drifted off to play. Sometimes they would all walk through the fields to Kilham. There was an old quarry on the way where they used to sit down for a rest.

"Tell us a story, Dan," they clamoured. "Tell us a ghost story!" And he would oblige with a chilling tale that had them spell-bound.

It seemed to go on forever, but it was only a matter of weeks before digs were found for the boys in Nafferton and they were sent to the village school, where lessons were on a more regular basis. By Christmas, many of the evacuees had returned home; there had been hardly any bombing in Hull and parents wanted their children back, even though they were advised against this by the authorities. Dan also was recalled. He spent Christmas with his family before starting a new job at Hall Road School the following term.

Dan found himself completely relaxed and happy during those early days at Pockthorpe Hall. This was the first time he had lived away from his family and he could do just as he wanted. He was freed from the pressures of school rules, of social rules, and the nagging worry about his sexuality. Here he could really be himself, a boy enjoying adventures with other small boys in an idyllic Never Never Land. But in the evenings when the children were asleep Dan Billany, the grown-up writer, surfaced. He was ready to start on a new project and this time it was going to be something completely different - a detective story. Dan had long despised such popular heroes of detective fiction as Lord Peter Wimsey and The Saint, but now he set out to create a rival, a man in a completely different mould. This was Robbie Duncan, an ex-jailbird who enjoys Keats and classical music, a superman who fights on despite horrific injuries, young, good-looking, completely unscrupulous, brilliantly clever, attracting danger and adventure at every turn.

The Opera House Murders opens in Granby House, a fine country mansion, flanked by horse-chestnut trees, and it is from the branches of one of these that a small boy collecting conkers witnesses a murder enacted on the road beneath him. A car pulls up, a bound and gagged man is dragged from the boot, laid in the road and the car is driven slowly forwards and backwards over the body, blood frothing and spurting beneath the wheels. This happens on the first page and the story continues in the same style, fast-moving and action-packed through to the last one. The chapter headings give a good idea of the content. Here are a few: Murder! Fair Women and Brave Men. Fun and Frolic at Dawn. I Admit Myself Kippered. The Characteristic Odour of a Rodent. Madam How and Lady Why.

Robbie Duncan, temporarily in residence at Granby House, as tutor to Jack, (the boy in the chestnut tree) comes to the rescue and battles his way through one tricky situation after another by a combination of his fine brain and brilliant physical prowess. Dan includes a romantic element in the person of Jack's widowed mother, an international opera singer who becomes Robbie's wife at the end of the book. But the main interest is the action, and who could ask for anything more dramatic and nail-biting. One could quote from almost any page, but take this as an example.

The road between Banham and Granby, as we know, was little used. Therefore it was surprising that when the mail van spun round a bend in the road nearer Banham than Granby, the postman should be confronted with an unmistakable corpse. He couldn't possibly have got past it without running over a head or a foot. It was a fat corpse, and as is the way with corpses, it made no attempt to minimise its bulk, or the component parts which made up that bulk. It was not even grave or serious as you would expect of death. Its belly stuck up like Melbreak. It did not lie cruciform, like little boys playing soldiers. Its limbs were thrown riotously about it, as if it had fairly rollicked into the arms of the dark angel. Its face was covered with mud. One arm was twisted under its body.

75

The postman stopped his van, slid out, uncurled, and somewhat timidly approached to inspect this empty Parcel, this Envelope which having carried its message, was thus cancelled and thrown ungratefully away in the road. And then a strange thing happened, a thing which baffled description. The Dead Man stirred. He stirred, he moved. He groaned very faintly. His twisted arm slid out from under him, almost. His eyelids flickered. The postman knelt and bent his head towards the Stirring Corpse. The corpse smiled and hit the head with a hammer. The hammer - ah, the wiles of men - had been in the hand that was twisted under the body.

Possibly Pockthorpe Hall was the inspiration for Granby House, but apart from that nothing in it bears any relation to Dan's life, or anybody else's for that matter. *The Opera House Murders* is pure escapism, just what was needed in those early days of the war, and it was an instant success. Faber and Faber snapped it up straight away and it was published in September 1940. The following March it appeared in America under the title *It Takes a Thief*. And it *was* a best seller. True, there were one or two critics who said unkind things like it wasn't realistic or that it was too violent, but the overwhelming majority were full of praise.

A really first-class he-man thriller writer such as Mr Billany is a valuable find in wartime when escape reading is at a premium. His thriller detective story is packed with action and murder and is one of the fastest-moving adventures we have ever read - definitely guaranteed to take your mind off anything but a direct hit. (The Sunday Times).

Mr Billany's style, light hearted, a trifle callous, semi-cynical fits perfectly the amoral people he is dealing with. If he can repeat this performance he will be the biggest discovery since Margery Allingham. "Billany for Villainy" should become Mr Faber's war-cry. (Manchester Evening News).

Does this mean I rank this as the best gooseflesher since Sherlock Holmes? Yes, I do. Fitzgerald will put himself on record and after you read it you'll agree. The title is *It Takes A Thief*, by Dan Billany. I'm not giving away any details except to say that scene after scene, with painful intensity and one killing after the other, rises to a climax when Detective Duncan digs up the treasure in the black of night and turns to meet the murderer ... It's grand and the kid has got It ... I'm breaking a rule and rating this one Grade AA — that's how good I know it is. So don't grab it today; get it within the hour. (Ed Fitzgerald, broadcasting on American radio).

At last Dan Billany was a real author, in print both sides of the Atlantic; there was a golden future ahead and a whole string of Robbie Duncan novels waiting to be written. There were even negotiations going on to sell the film rights; it seemed as if he need never look back. At 15 Lakeside Grove the family were bursting with pride and excitement. Harry couldn't wait to go round to Uncle

Mick's house to give him a copy.

***

But to resume the story of Dan's teaching career, one must go back to January 1940, before *The Opera House Murders* was published, although it was finished and Fabers had already shown an interest.

As a consequence of the phoney war, many of the evacuated children were now back home with their families in Hull, so staff were recalled to teach them, Dan Billany being one. He was assigned to Hall Road Senior Mixed School, newly re-opened, now that a full complement of air raid shelters had been built.

This school was about as different from Dan's old one at Chiltern Street as possible. Opened in 1935, it was set in its own playing fields on an eight acre site, and built on a series of quadrangles, with large windows making it light and airy. It was on the northern outskirts of the city catering for children from the new housing developments springing up there in the 1930s. Here Dan taught both girls and boys, aged eleven to fourteen, and at this school, teachers taught their own subjects, moving from class to class. There were specialist rooms for art, woodwork, science, cookery, music, and a well equipped library and gymnasium. But this was war-time and conditions were far from ideal. Two other Hull schools, Thomas Stratton and Wawne Street, whose own premises were in more dangerous positions near the railway and docks, were allocated to Hall Road. They used the buildings in the mornings, and the Hall Road pupils in the afternoons.

Dan quickly made a big impression on everyone, staff and children alike. He worked there for less than a year, but he was to be remembered and talked about for many years afterwards. His story-telling, his exuberance, his irrepressibleness marked him out. He was as unorthodox as ever in his attitude to the children, who were all fascinated by him, and took naturally to calling him Dan. His classes, naturally, were lively and noisy, with pupils encouraged to express themselves. And of course the headmaster, Mr Fenwick, disapproved but he failed to persuade Dan to change his ways. By this time he was full of confidence both in his teaching methods as well as his future as a writer.

Dan made an equally strong impact in the staff room, where he was well liked and his amusing conversation went down well with everyone. He enjoyed annoying the other chaps with his socialist views which he propounded vehemently and at length. They used to rib him about it and threatened to throw him out if he didn't shut up. But still he went on and on. So one day they carried out their threat. While one man held the staff room door open, two others took him by the shoulders and feet, and to cries of encouragement and laughter, they slung him out into the corridor, nor would they let him back in until the following day. The women had their own staff room at the other end of the school, which perhaps explains how the men could get away with such uninhibited behaviour.

For the young men it was hard to take school-life seriously. They were only marking time before joining up and going off to fight. No wonder that the men's staff room rang with laughter during the breaks. They played darts against the staff room notice-board, on a crudely drawn target, which often led to noisy disputes. Another boisterous game involved the men taking turns to throw a tennis ball at a penny in the middle of the table; whoever managed to knock it off kept the coin. Mr Isaacs was the unbeaten champion but Dan was an enthusiastic, if not altogether accurate player. They were never short of old tennis balls, as these were donated by Mr Hunter, a county tennis player. One of his favourite jokes was to balance a row of balls on top of the slightly opened staff room door and wait for someone to come in.

The staff at Hall Road were aware that Dan was a writer and they knew that his book *The Opera House Murders* was shortly to be published. He said he had written it during the long evenings of evacuation because there was nothing else to do in the country and that his landlady who had seen the manuscript had been scared witless! But at this time he was busy with a new idea, a children's book to be called *The Magic Door*. He had promised himself for some time that he would write up the stories of Standard Three's time travels, and this was the opportunity to do it. He repeated the format in his history lessons at Hall Road, developed the ideas and read draft chapters to his pupils. They loved it and later when it was published, eagerly tried to identify themselves with the characters in the book. In fact the boys in the story are clearly those from Chiltern Street, but the Hall Road staff and pupils felt that they had played their part in the genesis of the book, and were proud of its success.

After the war it became standard reading at the school and a whole new generation of children got to know and enjoy Dan Billany in the role of Mr Rocket. In the Art room, Mr Twiddy would introduce the new pupils to *The Magic Door* by reading from the beginning of Chapter 2.

There was a grinding kind of crash, shattering and heavy, and the green metal door slammed behind the schoolboys, and vanished from their sight; and strangely enough, each boy, as he looked round on the world at the other side, was gasping a little - for coming through the door gave them a curious feeling like going down very swiftly in a lift.

They were standing in a dark and tangled forest - a real forest, which made all the woods they had ever seen look like well-kept gardens. For the first time they understood how it was possible for the Babes in the Wood to lose their way; for the first time they began to have some sympathy with Hansel and Gretel.

Nothing could be seen but trees and bushes and tangled wild plants, whichever way they looked. Nettles, convolvuli, ivy, foxgloves, brambles, ragged bushes of every kind limited the view in every direction. They no longer knew where the Magic Door had stood by which they entered this new world. The forest was exactly the same all round them; there was no south, because the thick branches hid the sun, and so no north, east or west. They had no way of finding a path to anywhere. "Though that doesn't matter so much," thought Jack Crossley to himself; "not so much as you'd think, because after all we don't want to go anywhere."

The boys stood in a rather frightened silence for a minute, and then Fred Norman spoke.
"I've lost my glasses," he said.
That suggested a terrible thought to Alan Hope.
"Don't you lose that door-knocker," he said to Jack Crossley. "Else we'll never go back again, 'n' we'll have to stay in History all our lives."
Jack Crossley carefully put the knocker in his pocket.

Mr Twiddy's idea was to stimulate the children into producing some exciting art work, which they often did, but he could usually be persuaded to read on while they were working. The book was used as a stimulus in other lessons too, or just read aloud for fun. So in this way, Dan's teaching and influence continued for many years at Hall Road School.

Chapter 11

Into uniform

By the spring of 1940 Dan had decided to join the army. What motivated him to take such a step is a puzzle. He was far from being a man of action, not physically strong, nor well co-ordinated. On the contrary he was a rather frail, sensitive person, who one might have expected to be a pacifist. He hated the idea of pain and suffering and the concept of deliberately trying to hurt or even murder another human being must have been abhorrent to him. Nevertheless he did not hesitate to enlist.

Was it because all around him friends and colleagues were joining up? The majority of the men's staff room at Hall Road was already in uniform, as were Horace Mason, Reg Bloomfield and Jim Tanfield. No doubt Dan was swept along by the collective enthusiasm, eager to do his bit, to fight for his country which was at this time, at a very critical stage in the war. And certainly he had a political motivation; he had been fighting the tyranny of Fascism all his life, and although he had missed the Spanish Civil War, now he was offered the chance to be part of the action. But there was certainly a deeper motive, and Dan saw this, albeit subconsciously, as an opportunity to prove to himself that he was a man, to reach maturity at last and to escape the mantle of childhood which seemed to have been hanging over him for so long.

He passed his army medical in August 1940 and by the following October he was Private D Billany of "B" Company, Royal Army Service Corps, stationed at Sutton-in-Ashfield, Nottinghamshire. Dan was not suited to a life of soldiering at all and the rigours of army discipline came as a shock to him. He found the regime in many ways irksome, such as the absurdity of pre-breakfast kit inspection, every item folded just so and laid out in a precisely measured order. But worse was the physical training programme, the route marches, the drill with a heavy rifle and the cold wet nights under canvas. Regularly he collapsed in bed, falling asleep immediately, even when the lights were on and the rest of the Company were shouting and clumping around him. In his letters home Dan attempted to reassure the family that he was well, not needing anything ("don't bother w. any knitting") and that things would improve once the initial training period was over.

He admitted, in a letter to Eva, that the most disagreeable part of his new life was the absolute destruction of personal freedom ...

You're allowed to do exactly nothing unless you are told to do it. Holidays don't exist. Leave is negligible, a few days every six months. This means in fact that I shan't see anybody belonging to my old life till next Spring or Summer. You can't imagine how this feels. And as for taking up any of the threads, that can't be done while the war lasts. One has to accept the fact that the slate has been wiped clean. It is not easy to swallow this, I had a pretty bad time at first as I realised it; but now I am settling. I now understand Horace asking for news of "Jenkinson and the others in my dead life."

But there were some bright spots in the gloom. After few weeks military training he began to feel fitter and stronger. His corporal was a decent chap who could see no reason why Dan should not carry on typing his book. And soon Dan was happy to report that he was busy writing and had nearly finished his new Robbie Duncan story, *A Bell Shall Ring*.

By the end of October Dan had more good news to pass on to the family. *The Opera House Murders* was to be published in the United States under the title *It Takes A Thief* on very acceptable terms. Harpers, his U.S. publishers, and Fabers were eager to snap up his latest novel and, most exciting news of all, they were trying to sell the film rights.

Reviews of *The Opera House Murders* were still appearing in the press, Dan proudly quoted an extract in a letter to Eva:

"If this is a first novel, then Mr Billany must be a born story teller, for it has every mark of being the work of an author who is master of his trade ...... If there is one quality which Mr Billany has in a superb degree, it is that (of) making the fantastic seem real."

In spite of these encouraging developments in his literary career, Dan was still a private soldier, owned by the army, now based in Mansfield for driving training. He did not choose the job, as he explained in a letter home, "you do not choose in the army". After passing out as a driver in November 1940 Dan remained at Mansfield to take a map reading course. But he was already looking ahead and had applied for a commission with the Infantry which he felt he had a fair chance of achieving, backed by the Colonel's recommendation. He managed to snatch a few hours leave in Hull ("Bonzo went mad") but was disturbed to see the extent of the bomb damage in the city; this only increased his worries over Harry, Elsie and Joan.

In spite of the fact that he was virtually trapped in the army, Dan didn't think of himself as a soldier at all; he was first and foremost a writer, and was planning to continue writing in between military duties. By Christmas 1940, Dan had received Fabers' views on *A Bell Shall Ring*. This featured the villainous hero Robbie Duncan, whose earlier adventures his publishers were anxious to follow up. Dan had high hopes of the new book and he was confident that it would be accepted, even to anticipating the publication date. But in a long and detailed letter dated December 1940, T S Eliot of Fabers made serious criticism of *A Bell*

Shall Ring. He liked the title and the first few chapters but thereafter:

> ... your original inspiration flagged and you had to fill out the rest of the book with a great deal too much machinery of a kind that is rather out of date ... the 17th Century legend gave me forebodings: I think that this method of getting the reader all creepy was exhausted finally in The Hound of the Baskervilles, ... What I most regret about the later part of the book, however, is that the characters lose their human reality: especially Robbie himself, whose somewhat lawless but very attractive personality added so much to the Opera House. He might be almost anybody, ...

T S Eliot gives suggestions as to how the story could be improved, and in a final paragraph, writes:

> If I have been rather blunt, it is because I feel that if you are - as we hope - going on with the life and adventures of Robbie, this is a critical moment - the second and third books need especial care. From your address, I fear that you are unlikely to have much time to work on writing - but if and when you do, I shall be ready to push you to it with all the encouragement in my vocabulary.

There is no doubt that the poor reception of *A Bell Shall Ring* was a disappointment to Dan. He had been so confident and had buoyantly predicted "... my books show every sign of paying well". Dan began another book while he was at Sutton-in-Ashfield towards the tail-end of 1940 which he described as "peppy". Was this a Robbie Duncan novel? There is no trace of it ever having been given a title or submitted to Fabers for consideration.

By February, Dan had moved again, posted to the Infantry Training Centre of the Royal Warwickshire Regiment in Warwick. To his relief he heard that he had been accepted for a commission and in March he was transferred to No. 163 Officer Cadet Training Unit in North Wales. This was situated at Pwllheli, a small seaside town perched on the limb of the Lleyn peninsula. Dan was billeted in the Vyrnyw Hotel on the seafront. Although only sparsely furnished it was quite adequate, even "civilised", and a pleasing contrast to some of his other billets. For the four months they were in the camp, the young officers were kept hard at their training but in the evenings they enjoyed some free time. In Dan's case, much of this was used for writing.

In April he heard that Nelsons, the children's book publishers, had accepted *The Magic Door* and planned to bring it out in spring 1942. The manuscript had been passed to Nelsons by Jenkinson, Dan's tutor from the University College of Hull, with his recommendations. A busy exchange of letters between Dan and Mr Barringer of Nelsons began. It was agreed that Joan, now a student at Hull Art College, should provide a selection of illustrations for the book and that Dan should search for a new, bizarre title. He toyed with ideas such as "Let's Knock" or "Shall We Knock?" - not particularly inspired - and in the end decided to stick with *The Magic Door*.

Unfortunately Dan had received no spring royalties from *The Opera House Murders* nor had any money come through from his American publishers. He complained to Fabers, who responded with a placatory letter and encouragement to continue the Robbie Duncan series. But Dan had plenty of other projects on the go. He was hoping to close a deal with Harpers in the States for a collection of Robbie Duncan short stories. And there was the latest full length novel, the book begun the previous Christmas, although in a letter home Dan admitted that he had become bored with it. It was a pity about the lack of royalties, the money would have come in handy as Dan had ordered his officer's uniform and found that the £36 grant covered only half its cost. His pride in his appearance and refusal to compromise quality meant that he had to find the balance himself, luckily, he could just afford to do so. He proudly sat for the customary photograph, and sent copies to all the family. It is a typically posed composition, which shows him serious faced, peaked cap pulled well forward, nonchalantly holding his swagger stick. At this stage, he was hoping for an Army Education Corps commission which would mean "... a lecturer's job in London, a good rank and decent money ..."

In spite of a busy schedule, Dan and his fellow cadets still found time to socialise. Many local families whose own sons and daughters were enjoying hospitality far away were only too willing to welcome young soldiers into their homes. In this way Dan had already made friends in several of the places where he had been stationed, such as Harry and Marjorie Smith of Mansfield, who corresponded with him throughout the war. At their house he heard the boy soprano Denis Wright, who later, much to Dan's delight, had a great success as a soloist at a Promenade Concert under Sir Henry Wood.

It was at a musical evening in Pwllheli that Dan met Dorothy Warner, a slim, intelligent twenty year old who was living with her family at Ty-Du, a rambling farmhouse just outside the town. From the start they got on well. For once Dan seemed to have found a girl with whom he could relax and soon they had formed an easy-going relationship. When he mentioned her in his letters home, his family were delighted. Could this at last be the romance they had been hoping for? After all, Dan was twenty seven years old; it was about time he started courting. Probably he and Dorothy were no more than good friends, but for Dan to form an independent friendship with a woman was a big step in what many would consider to be the right direction. He had clearly rejected any thoughts of fulfilling his homosexuality. Dan was prepared to be unconventional, and passionately so about the things he believed in, but in this instance it seems he bowed to the general opinion that homosexuality was morally unacceptable. He makes this passing reference to the subject in a Robbie Duncan short story, written at about this time.

The love which animated both prose and verse was the sort of love which damns a person. I do not intend to be more specific. It did not damn the writer in my eyes, I had some sympathy with and for him, but it was a sort of love which, in the world as we know it, could not be made public. One might rather commit suicide; some have done.

Yet Dan was understandably nervous about embarking on a heterosexual relationship and allowed things to develop only slowly and comfortably between Dorothy and himself. The fact that the war was disrupting everyone's lives gave him a good excuse to avoid making any commitments.

Dorothy Warner lived with her parents and three younger brothers in a rented farmhouse to which they had moved when the bombing on London intensified. They were a very wealthy family. Harry Warner was a successful businessman who was one of the first to invest in the newly developing holiday industry. After the war, Warners Holiday Camps sprang up and flourished in a number of coastal resorts. Dorothy's family were most welcoming to Dan and it was not long before he had charmed them all. He was an entertaining and amusing talker on a wide range of topics including music, literature, and the theatre. (During his time in the army he wisely chose to be less vociferous about politics and religion.) He got on particularly well with Dorothy's three younger brothers, who loved his sense of humour and were most impressed by his theories on bringing up children with never a harsh word or hint of punishment. They were very noisy, boisterous lads, and Dan delighted in encouraging them in their high spirits.

The whole family was under Dan's spell, including Mrs Warner who mothered him and enjoyed cooking interesting dishes for such a hearty eater. He became a regular visitor at Ty-Du, pedalling out there on a borrowed bicycle as often as he could. He even entertained a fanciful hope that after the war he might take on the job of tutoring the three boys. The family seemed to know lots of influential people including members of the Government and at their house he met Billy Butlin, the holiday camp millionaire. Dan was moving on the edges of a society quite different from the limited confines of Lakeside Grove and Hull College, and he found it most agreeable.

However just as he was beginning to distance himself from his origins, to make new friends and find an independent life-style, fate pulled him back to the family circle in the most violent of circumstances. This was the telegram that he received.

CADET DAN BILLANY NO. 163 OCTU PWLLHELI NORTH WALES BOMBED OUT STOP MOTHER AND DAD IN HOSPITAL STOP COME QUICKLY STOP JOAN

Chapter 12
Heartbreak house

D an was granted compassionate leave and departed immediately for Hull, a long, anxious journey in war-time Britain when train timetables were in chaotic disorder. He found his sister Joan in a state of trauma, almost totally deaf, bewildered and incoherent. It was some time before she calmed down sufficiently to tell him the whole story.

On the night of April 25th 1941, the Luftwaffe had dropped two 40 cwt. parachute mines on the Gipsyville housing estate in West Hull, eight people were killed, four seriously injured and the area of damage covered 127 houses.

The Billanys were at home that evening when the siren sounded at twenty-five minutes past nine. They responded immediately - there had in the previous two months been some serious raids on the city - and went down the garden into the shelter. After a while Harry went outside fire-watching leaving Elsie and Joan in the shelter with Bonzo. There was silence for a long time so Joan followed her father. As she emerged into the pitch black garden she heard a faint whistling sound. "Is that incendiaries?" she called. "No," a neighbour shouted from the next garden, "it's a parachute mine - behind your house." And with that it went off. Joan heard no sound at all. She was thrown to the ground and the house started falling on top of her. In fact she was so near the side wall that much of the debris went over her and it was the blast that felled her. She couldn't breathe, there was a great pressure on her ears and chest and when the bricks stopped falling she got up and stumbled back to the shelter to find her mother.

She couldn't even find the shelter; the back garden was one huge pile of destroyed masonry. She bumped into her father who was staggering about, hands to his face which was pouring blood. An Air Raid Warden arrived and together they pulled away rubble from the front of the shelter and forced a way in. He lit a candle and by its light they could see Elsie. The top of her head seemed to be torn off and there were gaping wounds in her neck and chest. All Joan could whimper was "Please put the candle out." Her mother was conscious. She kept repeating "Joan, I'm dying, I'm dying," and Joan held her in her arms until the ambulance arrived and carried her away to hospital.

Joan's clothes were in tatters, virtually nothing remained of her skirt, and her shoes and socks had disappeared. A policeman came to help her into an ambulance, but she insisted on going back for Bonzo. They pulled him out of the rubble; he was rigid with fear but appeared to be unhurt, and the policeman carried Joan, still hugging the dog, into an ambulance. They spent the night together in the hospital and were discharged the next morning with no severe injuries.

85

Nevertheless, Joan was bruised and lacerated all over, numb with shock, and deaf from the explosion. She had no idea what had happened to her father.

She went initially to Uncle Mick's family; they lent her clothes and shoes and did their best to comfort her, but they were not able to cope with her mental suffering. Their house in River Grove had been on the edge of the same explosion, and when her cousin Tony had seen the remains of 15 Lakeside Grove the following morning, he had reported back to his family that no-one could possibly have come out of there alive.

Joan took Bonzo to Auntie Beattie and Auntie Doris's house in Spring Bank West, but by the following morning he had found his way back to Gipsyville. After that the two of them stayed close together and Bonzo was the one that saved Joan's sanity. They stayed temporarily with Joan's boyfriend, Ken, whose family had been evacuated to a village outside the city. She was wracked with headaches, subject to sudden black-outs and tormented by dreams, from which she would wake screaming in the night. She was very young, frightened and helpless with no-one to turn to. Relief came two and a half days after the disaster, when Dan arrived home and took charge.

Eventually, they found Harry, who had been taken to another hospital, suffering from severe facial injuries including a broken jaw; they were able to reassure him that Elsie was alive and recovering. In fact she was much worse than he was and suffered dreadfully during the months it took before she was well again. Both parents were moved to hospital in Leeds where they could receive the specialised treatment they needed. In spite of awful injuries, especially to Elsie, they both pulled through, but it was months before they came home. In one respect they were lucky. Had their accident happened a month later when the blitz was at its height in Hull, there were so many casualties that only the most basic of medical treatment could be given.

Dan's first problem was to find somewhere to live. He took Joan and Bonzo to Enid Mason's house. She was the wife of his friend Horace, now serving with the army, and she and her mother were living in Cottingham, on the outskirts of the city, in order to avoid the worst of the bombing. Their cat was not very welcoming to the new canine lodger, which was a pity because Bonzo liked cats, if only they would be friendly.

They went back to look at 15 Lakeside Grove which was nothing more than a heap of rubble. Dan found the old coal-bunker door, which years earlier, in their first smoke-free days, they had jokingly painted with roses and the name, HEARTBREAK HOUSE. In a final irony he stuck this like a signpost on top of the ruin. His old friend Reg Bloomfield helped him to salvage what he could. Dan's records and manuscripts were top of the list and some, but not all of them, were retrieved. In the amazing way of such things, they found several jars of bottled fruit, laid down by Elsie the previous summer, intact among the rubble. The council recovered the few possessions which had survived, such as Elsie's fur coat and a small chest of drawers which Harry had made; Joan had this in her bedroom at Enid's house.

Dan described the bombing of his family's home in precise detail in Chapter 15 of *The Trap*. The explosion itself is dramatic enough but the following chapter where Michael and Elizabeth visit her parents in hospital is pitiful in its simple statement of the awful facts. The fictional version is given extra bite as it includes the death of Elizabeth's thirteen year old brother, David, who was spending the evening with a neighbouring family when their shelter buckled in, killing them all. Dan restrains himself from laying blame for the tragedy at any particular door except for a few lines at the end of the chapter where his sadness and bitterness surface.

Over the bodies of children and old people the wolves are scrambling. Diplomatic wolves, who know all about oil concessions, international credits, trade routes, and a steady five per cent. The diplomatic wolves show their grinning, polite, pointed teeth. Over the bodies of children and old people.

Once in England, wolves' heads were worth a silver shilling.

It was vital for Dan to attempt, in the short time that remained, to find the family a house to rent, not an easy task with so many made homeless by the air raids. Added to this there was a huge bureaucratic maze to be negotiated with regard to compensation, an essential, but far from easy task for people who had lost everything. It proved impossible. Dan had to leave the accommodation problem unresolved when he returned to his unit in North Wales. Joan was still with Enid Mason in Cottingham, the remnants of the family possessions held in council warehouses.

★★★

Dan had been terribly shocked by what had happened to his family and never really got over the experience of seeing the three people he loved most crushed and all but destroyed. And he was haunted by the memory of his mother, swathed in bandages, in her hospital bed. Back in camp he was a changed man. This is how he described that time in *The Trap*.

Sometimes I saw my soldier-reflection in a mirror in the window of a confectioner nearby: I looked sad and puzzled, at this strange lost creature in new khaki, with his hair short and empty eyes.

But there was a way to make things go. After the first week, I took the army noisily. I told dirty stories, better dirty stories, funnier dirty stories than the ones I got in return, I chanted dirty songs when I shaved at reveille. I worked at P.T. as though it mattered. I was merry at all times. I was hearty. Meanwhile my soul crouched behind the barrage and hoped to get by.

Nevertheless, he fell back into his routine of training, writing and visiting the Warners. His already heavy correspondence load was increased by having to pester various bodies in pursuit of compensation and pensions for his parents, both still in hospital, and to encourage Joan in her search for a rented home in a relatively safe area. At the same time he was bombarding her with written instructions about the illustrations for *The Magic Door*. The original pictures, lost in the bombing, had to be redrawn. In spite of her injuries, the constant visits to Leeds and the pressures of everyday living in a city under nightly attack, Joan managed to produce a set of illustrations which surpassed her earlier attempt. Dan was delighted. He wrote to Joan, " ... colossal. They will just knock 'em over. Much better than the others which were lost." They were equally well received by Nelsons who described them as " ... a match for the book. i.e. unusual and by turns extravagant, amusing, crude, incredible and brilliant." At last *The Magic Door* was all but finished.

The final weeks of Dan's course at Pwllheli passed by in a frenzy of concentrated effort; the officers were kept at it almost continuously, marching, manoeuvring and lying in wet fields for twenty eight hours at a time, a regime unhelpful to a writer whose publisher was pressing for a new book. Meanwhile, his agent was negotiating the sale of his short stories and had also submitted his radio play *A Hitch in Time* to the BBC. The plot, set in a thinly disguised Beverley, hinged on the not-quite-synchronised chiming of two church clocks. As usual Dan was confident that it would be accepted but was again to be disappointed. The BBC must have seen some promise in the play, however, for they asked him to submit any further work. Despite this latest setback and the rejection of *A Bell Shall Ring*, Dan never lost his optimism and always believed that he could produce material that would sell. He continually looked ahead, had new ideas and in his letters home he said he had "... irons in the fire, and I hope they will get nice and hot soon".

On 5th July 1941 Dan completed his training and was appointed to an Emergency Commission as Second Lieutenant in the East Yorkshire Regiment. The brief leave period which followed was spent with Joan, helping her move into the bungalow she had found in Jesmond Road, Cottingham. Several bits of furniture salvaged by the council from Lakeside Grove were delivered, including the wrong sewing machine, which Joan stubbornly left out in the garden for three months. Harry and Elsie Billany were discharged from hospital and joined Joan and Bonzo at the bungalow, but neither of them ever really recovered from the bombing. Harry, aged 54, never worked again and for the rest of his life, suffered from a debilitating heart condition.

For a short time Dan was stationed at the Regimental HQ, Beverley, near enough to be able to help the family in Cottingham. He also managed a meeting with Dorothy who was now serving with the WRAC at Richmond in North Yorkshire. He borrowed a car and they drove out into the country. It was a lovely summer's day and for them both a brief respite from the demands of army life and communal living.

At the beginning of August, Dan was on the move again, this time to Helston in Cornwall. Eva was living in Lincolnshire, where she had been evacuated with her school early in the war. She had settled in Bourne where she married another evacuated school-teacher, Charles Wilkin. Shortly after, he was recalled to his job in Hull, but they thought it safer that Eva, now pregnant, should stay in the relative safety of Lincolnshire, with Charles' parents for company. So by the summer of 1941, the Billany family which had always been so close were separated and rootless. Dan was in Helston, Eva was in Bourne and Joan and her parents were convalescing in Cottingham.

Dan took his responsibility as head of the family very seriously; there was a constant stream of letters between the three locations, letters reassuring them and planning for the future. His first concern was to find more suitable accommodation for Joan and his parents. Wales or Cornwall seemed the safest place and, with help from his friends the Warners, he was negotiating the rent of a farm cottage in the Pwllheli area, when an offer came from Eva to have them to live with her. The only problem was money, but Dan smoothed this over and arranged to send Eva a regular sum for household expenses, so in the autumn of 1941 they moved to Lincolnshire.

Dan's first taste of life as an officer was in Cornwall with the 7th Holding Battalion of the East Yorkshire Regiment. This was a full battalion living under canvas in the woods and countryside near Helston. Its sole function was to train and supply troops as replacements for the East Yorkshires. He took command of a platoon, thirty men in all, and proceeded to lead them in their training, although he was just as much a beginner himself, and not enjoying it one bit. It was a summer and autumn of teeming rain. He wrote home:

> Whenever I wake in the night - which isn't often, what with the work - I hear the rain beating on the canvas of our tent. Everything is damp and smelly - our tent is in a little wood - and we wash in canvas bowls.

Dan endeavoured to get to know the men in his command. He viewed them in a similar light to the boys in his class at Chiltern Street, himself the teacher drawing them out and leading them on by sympathy and understanding. In the event, there was little opportunity to do more than learn a few names as they were kept hard at work, officers and men alike. Dan had no patience with military discipline or routine. The pettiness of what seemed to be nonsensical orders, the lack of any sympathy or understanding of weaknesses, and the immature behaviour of his fellow officers were a constant source of irritation. At the same time they were all being put through a punishing physical regime, much of it carried out in the pouring rain.

By September 1941, Dan had been appointed Battalion Education Officer which as he wrote to Eva, sounded important but didn't mean a lot, except that he was excused some military work. To Dan's delight, his old friend Horace Mason, also a newly commissioned officer, was posted to Helston at about this time. They had kept in close touch by letter, and through Horace's wife Enid, who had taken Joan in when she was homeless. Dan had always valued the Masons' opinions and often given them manuscripts to read, so he was very pleased to resume the friendship and the discussions, particularly on literary topics. Horace, like Dan, was an academic, a thinker rather than a man of action, so it is not surprising to find the two of them enjoying musical evenings at the home of the Headmaster of the Secondary School, where they had a standing invitation to supper. These were a special pleasure to Dan; he wrote:

> ... we were there last Saturday - two pianos, a radiogram, stacks of good records, and his wife can play Beethoven like Paderewski, also some of his teachers go in, and we have grand sing-songs, all bellowing Handel and Schubert round the piano. He is a very decent chap, left wing - so is all his staff.

Letters from Fabers began to reach Dan at his far-flung posting: what did he think of a cheap (9d.) edition of *The Opera House Murders*? Not much apparently, which was just as well since less than six weeks later Fabers had to withdraw their offer - the paper shortage was beginning to bite. Despite this, Mr Stewart held out hopes of a new Robbie Duncan thriller for publication in Spring 1942, but Dan was finding it almost impossible to fit writing into his busy schedule and had to put him off.

He still kept in touch with Jack Crossley, now aged twelve, and asked T S Eliot for a signed copy of *Old Possum's Book of Practical Cats* for him. Eliot was happy to send one but could not resist a gentle prod at Dan as he enquired whether "your duties have at least allowed you to ponder a new thriller for us, even if not to write it?"

Things were not going too well for the Billany family in Lincolnshire. It was a claustrophobic situation in a fridge of a house with a chronic shortage of money and the constant drone of bombers passing and repassing overhead. Joan was slowly recovering but the strain of the past months was telling, and she and Eva, now heavily pregnant, were often at loggerheads. Joan realised that the set-up at Bourne could not continue and asked Dan's advice; he suggested she find a job, the sooner the better, before the army claimed her. So Joan went to the local Labour Exchange, where she was offered a job in Yeovil, 250 miles away, as a tracer at Westlands Aircraft Factory. She left immediately, found lodgings in the town, and although she was terribly homesick and cried constantly for two weeks, she stuck at it and before too long made friends at work and life became bearable.

Dan's reaction to the news of Joan's job was delight in her new-found confidence. He wrote her an elder-brotherly letter of concern and approval, with perhaps a hint at the end that he was finding army life heavy going.

I know what it feels like at first on a new job away from home, but I'm very glad you're doing it; it will do you a great deal of good to know that you depend entirely on what you earn, and to feel in control of your own finances and your own life ... it's in your own hands to stick it or not, as you feel inclined; in the army, on the other hand you have to stick it. I must come over as soon as possible and look at your digs.

Everyone seemed to be moving south. The Warners had left their farm in North Wales for a village only six miles from Portsmouth, an odd move in view of the south coast bombing and invasion scares. Dan, worried that Joan might feel left out on a limb, drew her a sketch map of the west country complete with matchstick men, which showed the relative positions of himself in Cornwall, Joan at Yeovil, the Warners at Rowland's Castle near Portsmouth, Jenkinson his former tutor in Devon and Ken, Joan's boyfriend, now living in Bristol. He urged Joan to spend weekends with the Warners.

Dan had come to a decision in the weeks before Christmas which he feared would disturb his parents: he was determined to apply for overseas service. In his own words, he was "sick as hell of standing at the side of everything and not getting in somewhere", he felt it was time he stepped out. Horace Mason was now on a draft for India and Dan decided he should follow him or, if it worked out that way, precede him. India was as safe as England, he reassured his parents, maybe safer. And anyway, he wrote, it was very unlikely that the war would last until Christmas 1942 and might even be over by next April. It was a chance to see the world.

Why was Dan so determined to do this? Was he really looking for adventure? Possibly, but in view of his disinclination for army discipline and physical hard work, it seems a strange decision. Maybe Horace's resolve to serve overseas was his spur, but it was more likely that Dan's strong sense of responsibility told him that it was his duty to fight, that if anyone had to be sacrificed in the action, then he must at least take his chance. He was fully aware of what he was going to; the reassurances in the letter were intended for the family only.

Early in 1942 he learned that his draft had come through and preparations for embarkation began. Dan was excited at the prospect, keen to be involved at last, though he was worried about the family. He was still working, rather dispiritedly, on *A Bell Shall Ring*, and although *The Magic Door* was finished, there were hitches in its publication which were frustrating. Nevertheless, he planned to take his typewriter and continue to write whenever there was a lull in the action.

His embarkation leave was a raw weekend in February spent at Eva's house in Bourne, where his parents were still living. Old friends from Hull joined them for the send-off, including Jack Crossley. The only one who it seemed would miss the party was Joan. Her employers in Yeovil refused to give her time off; the war effort must come first, they said. She was determined to be there, so she defied authority and the aircraft industry and caught the next train east. The family was complete for their last few days together.

Chapter 13

Sea and sand

Dan left England in mid-February 1942, on board the *Mauretania*, a former Cunard cruise liner, now commandeered as a troopship, painted a dull grey and crammed to its limits with 4500 men and their equipment. There was a wonderful send-off. Dan received telegrams of good wishes from many friends, including Stewart, his editor at Fabers and all the members of the Warner family. But he did not know where he was going. In fact the ship was bound for Suez, carrying reinforcements for the North African campaign. It was to be a six week voyage, via the west coast of Africa and round the Cape.

Dan was concerned at the appallingly crowded conditions in which the men lived, sleeping in hammocks slung closely together below decks. As for the officers, life on board ship was very pleasant. He wrote home enthusiastically about the food and accommodation.

I wish you could have the food we get on here; grapefruit, oranges, apples every day, plenty of eggs, bacon, fish, chicken, duck, turkey, beef, mutton (they call it lamb) and everything you can imagine, including ices, champagne and so on. Everything is quite super; I have hot and cold water in my cabin, and a Vi-Spring mattress. We can buy as much chocolate as we like.

To the family back in England, subsisting on war-time rations, this was indeed extravagant living. But for all the opulence of his surroundings, Dan soon began to feel the stirrings of homesickness. He wrote to his parents:

England, bleak and wintry, is still England - my own country, and when I see the sun climbing higher and higher up the sky each day although it is February, I don't really enjoy the heat as I used to enjoy summer in England. One rather feels that something's gone wrong, that the sun shouldn't be as high as that or the water so blue, and that the world is out of joint.

The leisurely pace of life on board ship meant that Dan felt motivated to start a new Robbie Duncan thriller and following a surge of ideas he had begun what he hoped would be a "smasher" called *Whispering* or *The Young Lady's Hand*. He felt confident that given an undisturbed month he would make a good job of it. Approximately three weeks into the voyage, he was still working on the book. Although his typewriter was broken Dan had managed to carry on using the services of a stenographer on board and had completed chapter seven. But by this time, he found that *Whispering* was being pushed into the background. The unfinished manuscript which eventually found its way back to the Billany family shows the same racy style of his earlier work.

What had caught his imagination was his role of officer to the men of his draft, which numbered almost a hundred. Once again they brought out the schoolteacher in him; he thought of them as his lads, quickly learned their names, their backgrounds and in many cases their problems. In such a restricted area there was little opportunity for training so during the weeks at sea the officers' main job was to keep the men occupied, in particular to steer them away from gambling and drinking. From 8.30 a.m. when he took them for PT on the top deck, through the day until bedtime, Dan was continually "fussing round them" (as he wrote). The men had nothing to do in their cramped quarters all day but smoke and play cards, so to help pass the time, Dan organised activities such as darts tournaments, debates, sing-songs and concerts up on the deck.

I shall always remember these concerts, ... the men crowded silently on the decks, the cigarette-smoke, and a figure standing on the hatches, a voice singing "The Rose of Tralee" - romantically incongruous, the English voice, the khaki drill clothing, and the full African moon.

There were discipline problems of course but Dan, as one might expect, did his best to deal with them fairly and sympathetically. In a letter he describes how a young soldier, very drunk, tried to fight him late one night in the pitch dark of the top deck.

He said he wanted to go on a special sick report, and maintained "Nobody can deny me a spesh'l sick r'port." I got him to sit down, and he burst into tears, and sobbed for about ten minutes, saying he knew he'd got consumption, that was why he was so thin. There were some people helping me with him, but two of them were drunk as well, and weren't much use. I got him asleep, and was just putting his blankets round him when he got up to fight me. Later, after wandering round the ship, he got up on a liferaft to throw himself overboard, but we got him down all right.

Dan found himself so involved in this life that he admitted he had not been so happy for years. He had begun to notice an improvement in the men under his command, and reckoned that with another six months at sea his draft would be transformed.

When Dan wrote about his war experiences in *The Trap*, a fictionalised account featuring Lt. Michael Carr, he invented a group of men, members of Carr's platoon, who went through the action together, from the camp at Helston to capture in the desert. These characters are developed as the story progresses and their relationships with Lt. Carr form a key element in the novel. One particularly troublesome recruit is Frank Shaw. He is eighteen but looks thirteen, thin and undernourished with a defiant attitude towards authority. He had spent some periods of the last two years in military prisons for various offences. Lt. Carr realises that Shaw's problems are mostly related to his immaturity and tries to help the lad by encouragement and understanding. An incident on the voyage in which Shaw gets blind drunk and bellicose seems to be based on the young drunk in Dan's letter. This troublesome soldier was just the type of misfit with whom Dan could sympathise, the sort he had already met in the classroom. He wrote of Shaw, in *The Trap*:

> The prison bars of the last two years had left scars on his soul. Caging a child. The cruelty of it was medieval. He was a fool: but the answer to folly is not wickedness. We must not torture children when they are slow to grow up.

We do not know the fate of the boy who was Dan's model for Shaw, maybe he suffered the same end as the fictitious Shaw, which was to be shot by a German rifleman only minutes after surrender.

★★★

Eventually the ship passed Aden and entered the Red Sea, reaching Suez a day later. The six weeks at sea had been merely an interlude, Dan was back in the real world and for him the war was about to begin. They disembarked at Port Tewfik and travelled by train to an Infantry Base Depot. Dan described the strange journey westwards along the Egyptian coastline.

> The train, when it came, reminded me of the one which climbs Snowdon by the track railway. The coaches were not subdivided into compart-ments, but were like an old-fashioned English tram. Seats were wooden, and windows without glass. If you wanted to keep out of the raw night air you pulled up a slatted wooden shutter. There were no lights whatever. We were tired, cold and subdued as we crowded in. The men were docile. A strange, unfriendly, hopeless sort of rail journey, in a primitive train, at night, and in a foreign land. No voices calling 'goodbye', no hands wav-ing from the platform. One's heart was bruised, empty and numb. The moonlight showed us glimpses of Suez as we moved out: white Eastern buildings with tall, thin, knobbly spires to them, all drenched in the white moonshine, all still and silent, but a chink of light appearing occasional-ly from an Arab eating-house.

The description comes from the *The Trap*, as do the other quotations in this and the following two chapters. There is no doubt that here Dan was recording his own experiences in the Middle East.

At length, the train halted at what appeared to be nowhere. Nothing but desert and the distant hills in pitch blackness. The men were assembled and marched to the camp, fed and settled into tents. Dan slept in the Officers Mess and next day took stock of the place he had come to. This was the Base Camp at

Quassassin. There were 50,000 men here, camped in the desert in thousands of tents, row upon row, awaiting transfer to the front line. Dan was not impressed with what he saw.

> They told me this was the best place in the Middle East outside the Delta. To me, after the luxury of the trip out, and with English thoughts in my head, it was simply the wilderness. There was a bright black road, straight as a spear, through the area: military trucks and vehicles roared along it, keeping always to the right. On one side, parallel to the road and a mile from it, ran the wall of brown bare hills: on the other side, the Bitter Lake. Our vast dispersed camp straddled the road, between the hills and the water; tiny tents lost on the empty face of the sand. You could walk many miles along the road without leaving the camp. In the camp were canteens run by the Egyptian NAAFI, every one just like every other one: there were two cinemas, two miles apart: there were tiny stalls (watchmakers, confectioners, whatnot) with Egyptians behind the counter. There was a wooden shack which was the Church of England, and a wooden shack which was the Ottoman Bank. Down towards the Bitter Lake there was a tiny, filthy, biblical Egyptian village which did not appear to have been emancipated from the Plague of Flies. Apart from these things, there was nothing nothing nothing nothing except khaki khaki khaki khaki, sand sand sand sand and flies flies flies flies.

In a letter to his family dated 4th April (sent via Auntie Beattie in Hull as his parents were in the process of moving to Yeovil) Dan attempted to reassure them that he was well and safe but after travelling 10,000 miles was unable to tell them more than after a weekend in Scarborough.

The days at Base Camp were spent in training, running over the dusty desert and up the low craggy hills under the beating sun. Sometimes they swam in the Bitter Lake, if their sunburn allowed. In due course, his posting came through and Dan joined a train early one morning which made its way laboriously westwards through the rich cultivated land of the Nile Delta. Dan was shocked by the living conditions of the Egyptian peasants, the filthiness of their villages, their desperate poverty. He writes in pity and anger for these "withered wretches", paid far below a living wage and treated worse than slaves by the rich landowners, then only to be mocked and despised by the Allied soldiers who called them "dirty Wogs".

They halted long enough to have a walk around the former holiday resort of Mersa Matruh on the Egyptian coast. The town was deserted, silent and eerie, glass gone from the windows and sand sifting into the empty rooms. Most of the buildings had been smashed by bombs, but what filled Dan with quiet horror was the dead silence of this place.

The next stage of the seemingly endless journey was again by rail, this time in cattle trucks, ten officers per truck, the men more crowded. The little train jerked and jolted its way across the desert to the transit camp at Fort Capuzzo, sited on one of the ancient desert trackways, which had featured in the previous months of to-and-fro battles. They crossed into Libya, left the train and spent two nights camped out at this desolate dot on the map of nowhere; here they suffered the first desert dust storm, referred to by the men as a "shit-storm", a miserable and frequently repeated experience.

... the sand blew right in on us, and when we woke in the morning our eyes, ears and nostrils were full of sand. But the men were under odd fly-sheets and scraps of canvas, which the screaming wind sometimes plucked off the desert's face like an old dry piece of sticking-plaster. The yellow fog of dust was everywhere. We could not see more than a couple of yards ahead at the best, and had to tie handkerchiefs over our faces in order to breathe.

Transfer to the front was by 3-ton army lorry. There were no roads, the vehicles bumped along old camel trails, made wider and wider by constant traffic avoiding the original track, now worn-down and rocky. There was nothing to look at; apart from sand and stones, the only things visible were burnt-out tanks and trucks, reminders of earlier clashes, some with "TT" crudely painted on their sides; this was a sign that the Tyne Tees Division had passed through. The only thing Dan recalled about the journey was stopping at a junction of several tracks in the sandy wilderness and seeing a board with the name "Piccadilly" painted on it.

Imagine: - A single wooden signboard with crude lettering, PICCADIL-LY CIRCUS: and nothing else at all - round the grooved wheel-ruts, round the up-ended barrel or the dozen cairns of brown stones that marked the place, the lone and level sands stretch far away. You stand by your truck, in the shadow of the signboard, and you are wrapped entirely in the everlasting silence of the sand. Piccadilly Circus. Not a movement anywhere under the blue bowl of the sky. The bare brown desert is still and empty, to the horizon.

Chapter 14
Into the cauldron

When Italy declared war upon France and Britain on 10th June 1940, aligning herself with Nazi Germany (in fulfilment of the pacts of 1936 and 1939), a whole new field of war was opened in North Africa. After the Fall of France in 1940, no help to contain Italian colonial ambitions could be expected from the French colonies which were now administered by the Pro-German Vichy Government, in fact the reverse was probably the case and they were expected to support Italian territorial expansion plans. The Italian army commanders were under Mussolini's orders to create a 'New Roman Empire' and as a first step, to take Egypt and the Suez canal.

The two Italian possessions in North Africa, Libya and Ethiopia were safely 'contained' by the French colonies of Morocco, Algeria and Tunisia in the west and in the east by British Egypt. Not that Egypt was a British colony but the Egyptians allowed Britain to site military and naval bases on its territory, although the young King Farouk and his advisors were somewhat fickle in their support of Britain and needed to be continually reassured and encouraged by the Foreign Office. A force of 86,000 men was garrisoned in Egypt, under General Wavell, whose command extended beyond North Africa and into the Middle East, Cyprus and British East Africa.

Scarcely a day had passed after the declaration of hostilities between Britain and Italy when the first shots were heard. A group of highly trained British mobile forces attacked the static Italians and then continued to press them, supported by the RAF who bombed airfields and naval installations in Tobruk. Mussolini desperately needed a victory to bolster up his credibility with Hitler and therefore exerted pressure on the Libyan Army Commander, Graziani, to mount an attack on targets in Egypt as soon as possible. Despite il Duce's demands, General Graziani did his best to defer any attack on the quite legitimate grounds that his forces were not ready. But eventually he had to give way and agreed to begin the assault on Egypt in September 1940.

Graziani and his men fought their way eastwards into Egypt as far as Sidi Barrani, where they stopped. General Wavell did not counter-attack at once, preferring to delay his offensive until he was good and ready, so it was not until December 1940 that the British troops, well supported by tanks and artillery, drove the Italians out of Sidi Barrani. Heavy fighting continued intermittently into the new year and by the end of January, Tobruk was in Allied hands. By early February, 180,000 enemy prisoners had been taken and Wavell's men had advanced as far west as Beda Fomm.

In Berlin, Hitler sourly observed these events and decided, with reluctance as he had other more pressing plans, to send a German force in a supporting role to assist his struggling ally. Rommel, with two armoured divisions, was dispatched to the Western desert.

The effectiveness of the German troops increased rapidly as they gained experience and confidence in the handling of their armour in desert warfare conditions. This caused great concern to the Allied leaders who were devastated to find that the new British tanks were proving unsuited to the desert and their crews untrained in their use.

In June 1941 it was decided to replace General Wavell with General Auchinleck, who launched 'Operation Crusader' in November. The 4th Battalion of the East Yorkshires, newly diverted from Cyprus, was in the thick of this and immediately engaged in battle. The Allies captured 70,000 Italians and pushed as far west as Agedabia. Action continued until January 1942, only ending when both sides fell back exhausted, but it was considered to be a definite Allied victory.

The British Eighth Army had suffered great losses during 'Crusader' yet the war leaders found themselves unable to supply more troops and replacement weapons. The men and equipment destined for the Western Desert had to be diverted, even when already en route to Egypt, to the Far East. Here the situation was desperate. Following their successful attack on Pearl Harbour, the Japanese had overwhelmed Thailand, Malaya, Borneo and even Hong Kong; Singapore was about to fall and the invasion of Burma was imminent.

The Allied Command realised just how much the Eighth Army was weakened and needed time to re-group, but mistakenly believed that Rommel's forces were in the same state. Even though losses in men and equipment in the Afrika Korps were greater than the Allied losses, Rommel's force was not nearly as spent at the Allies believed. Morale was high, helped by welcome deliveries of tanks and fuel; Rommel felt that there was no time like the present to launch an attack and this he did. Benghazi fell and he was within reach of Tobruk by February. The enemy was preparing for the next great offensive south of Gazala.

Such were the positions of the embattled armies when Dan joined the 4th Battalion of the East Yorkshire Regiment in April 1942.

★★★

Dan was assigned to "C" Company under Major Huddleston, who was surprised to learn that a new lieutenant was on his way, but any extra personnel was welcome so he detailed Dan to take command of a platoon under temporary supervision of a sergeant. The men in this platoon were tough, desertworthy soldiers, many of them dockers or fishermen from Hull. Most had been in North Africa for the best part of a year and were well used to living and fighting in such inhospitable conditions. Dan felt raw and inexperienced beside them.

98

The Battle of Gazala: May - June 1942

Showing the Allied system of 'boxes', a series of strong-points protected by minefields, on a line approximately 50 miles long running from Gazala to Bir Hacheim.

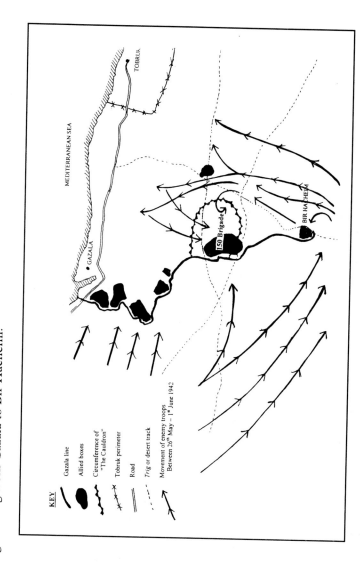

KEY

	Gazala line
	Allied boxes
	Circumference of "The Cauldron"
	Tobruk perimeter
	Road
	Trig or desert track
	Movement of enemy troops Between 26th May – 1st June 1942

MEDITERRANEAN SEA

TOBRUK

GAZALA

150 Brigade

BIR HACHEIM

Nevertheless he called them all together for an initial talk at which he introduced himself in his own inimitable way.

Dan leaned back against a jeep as the men of his platoon grouped themselves around him. He smiled encouragingly at them.

"At ease, lads," he said and the platoon shuffled their feet in the dust. "Well I'm your new platoon commander. I'm from Hull just like most of you." He smiled again but received no friendly response; the men stared back at him straight faced.

"You are all old hands out here and I'm new to the desert - and to running a platoon, come to that, - so I hope I can count on you to put me right if necessary. We're in this together, living and fighting together but not, I hope, dying together!" He paused but there was no flicker of amusement.

"And as we're all in it together, I want you to think of me as your pal rather than your officer. I don't expect you to call me 'Lt. Billany' or 'Sir', my name's Dan. So, please just call me Dan."

The platoon, accustomed to the strictest of army standards, was shocked. Was this the man who would lead them into battle? Heaven help them all.

Major Huddleston received another surprise when an agitated sergeant reported Dan's instructions to the men - "Call me Dan." The Major was as appalled as his informant. What sort of an officer have I got here? he wondered, as he reprimanded Dan and made it clear that this unorthodox behaviour was not acceptable.

The 4th Battalion East Yorks, together with the 4th and 5th Battalions of the Green Howards formed the 150 Brigade, a fighting force of about 1000 men who occupied a "box", that is an area of desert roughly one mile square, on the Gazala Line. This was not a fortified defence line in the sense of the Maginot Line but a series of self-contained strong-points, defended on all sides and protected by minefields and barbed wire, which were strung out on a line stretching approximately fifty miles from Gazala on the coast down to Bir Hacheim, the most southerly box.

Between the Allied boxes and in front of Rommel's army ran a long strip of land, north to south, which varied in width from 100 yards to two miles. This was heavily mined. Narrow passages through the minefield were marked with trip wires which were patrolled by roving Allied armoured units.

Rommel's deployment of his armoured units was radically different from that of the Allied Forces. The latter believed they should operate independently of each other, the units being spread thinly over the whole Gazala area with the idea of supporting the infantry dug in within their boxes. The German commander considered that the only chance of success in desert warfare conditions lay in highly mobile armoured units, used as a mass attack force and not piecemeal.

The 150 Brigade commanded by Brigadier Haydon occupied a box situated at Rotunda Ualeb, between the old desert tracks of Trig Capuzzo and Trig el Abd and over ten miles to the north of the last box held by the Free French at Bir

Hacheim. The orders to 150 Brigade were to defend the minefield with fire. They must prevent the enemy engineers lifting the mines in order to make gaps for their motorised forces to move through. The Brigade must hold its position until the expected support force of tanks should arrive. Dan's platoon was engaged in the protection of the eastern edge, facing away from the enemy. Major Huddleston had had time to observe Dan more closely and although he recognised his willingness, realised that this man was not a natural soldier. So, he had wisely positioned the inexperienced Lt. Billany in what he expected would be the rear of the action.

So extensive were the minefields on all sides of the box that any movement by vehicle was extremely hazardous. The front line troops also had the job of patrolling the desert, at night, searching for German recognisance groups. Dangerous though this was, the men liked the excitement as a relief from the boredom of routine training.

Dan's platoon was engaged in 'digging-in', an essential operation. It proved particularly difficult as their bit of the desert was solid rock under a covering of about twelve inches of sand. This meant back-breaking work with pick-axes in the hot dry desert sun. There was a brief visit from two men from the Royal Engineers with pneumatic drills, but they didn't stay long enough to have much effect on the rock barrier. The first job was to dig pits for the Bren Guns and a narrow slit trench for every two riflemen; next came the men's 'bivvy holes' where they lived and slept, these were usually six foot square and four foot deep. Bivouac sheets were then stretched over the top, camouflaged with nets and sand held down with iron pegs. Although the Germans regularly flew recognisance flights over the Gazala area, observing and photographing, the company positions were still very difficult to see by ground troops. Dan's men stayed with their initial diggings-in for several weeks, into May 1942.

★★★

Spring in the desert is an unpleasant season. The Kham-sihn, a hot, dust-carrying wind came over in the afternoons, lifting the dust like a heavy cloud formation rising from the horizon. As the dust storm approached, heralded by a thin screaming noise, the men rushed to cover weapons and food, and then to hide in their bivvies. Even when the storm was not upon them the dust still got everywhere: hair, food, water, bedding, weapons; rarely was there no wind at all. Dan's poem, written eight years earlier in the deserted graveyard at Leven seems to presage the experience.

> See, often in a day of blustering heat,
>   The angry wind storms down upon the dust
>   Whirling it so, with parched, vindictive gust,
>   That wreathed dust-spectres stalk along the street.

101

The desert was a place of extremes. From nine o'clock the heat came on and beat down until about four when it began to lose its fierceness and by seven it was dark. Nights were cold and raw with a damp fog which soaked clothes. It was a place fit for war - and nothing else.

The routine of the day began early before the intense heat. Breakfast was usually a tinned meal, sausages or bacon with biscuits, sometimes porridge, but always washed down with plenty of tea. Then the work of the platoon started: training or digging until noon when the sun and heat became unbearable. After tiffin, it was siesta time until four. The men would lie in their bivvies, too hot and sweaty to sleep but at least resting. Work restarted as the day cooled, a cooked meal was produced at seven, platoon officers checked that each man's water bottle was full, and stand-to was from 8.30 to 9.30.

To their surprise, the men found the desert had an active animal population, for instance, the famous jerboa or desert rat and also some insects and spiders of unpleasant size and habits. Some of the men kept chameleons as pets in their tents, they were wonderful fly killers; sometimes they would sit on a shoulder and ride as their owners walked about the camp. Ticks worked their way under a man's skin, causing a nasty sore; the entirely hairless spiders were as large as mice; scorpions hid in army boots. Dan describes one of these in a letter as "a bloody big yellow bugger like a nasty kind of lobster ... the men threw one on the fire and it burst with a loud pop". But the flies were the worst, ever-present in immense swarming clouds, appearing out of nowhere and settling on food, skin, everything and *biting*.

In these unpleasant conditions, the platoon developed a cohesion. Although this was brought about more by circumstances than Dan's ability to command, he was pleased to see how close his group of men had become.

> We lived so very much under each other's eyes; our lives were common property. Similarities and the dropping of protective reserve endeared man to man. So many of our old, complicated, sophisticated reactions were not needed, and fell away. We talked to each other with the understanding frankness of some children. And we did not talk much. There was no chattering. Our lives were steady and taciturn, like those of farm workers.

★★★

By the middle of May, all the platoon was well dug in and concealed when orders were received to cancel training and concentrate on defence work. German tanks had been observed on the move. A week passed without further disturbance and then came a warning from 8th Army Headquarters of an expected full-scale attack.

On the evening of 26th May, Rommel began moving his panzer divisions and a large force of tanks in a south easterly direction towards the Bir Hacheim box.

At the same time a much smaller force was despatched towards the north as a decoy. He sent an Italian division to attack the Free French box itself and swung the main mass of his forces round Bir Hacheim and continued to the north. Some of these troops engaged the 201 Brigade in their 'Knightsbridge' box which lay approximately eight miles east of 150 Brigade.

By lunchtime on 27th May, many skirmishes had taken place as the German and Italian mobile columns met units of Allied forces. Although Rommel's troops scored some successes it was not altogether one-sided and to their leader's concern they had sustained serious losses in men and tanks. During the afternoon, the Germans met with increased resistance. On this same day Dan and his platoon were busy digging new positions in 150 Brigade box, a matter of urgency since the desert was extremely flat in this area and his men were visible from miles away; but it was very slow and arduous, pick-axing the rock in the searing heat.

The next day it seemed both sides were getting their breath back. Rommel was busy touring his forces, assessing the situation and issuing orders. He discovered that he had been awarded a bonus in that his engineers had managed to cut through the minefield at Trig El Abd, south of 150 Brigade box, thus allowing essential ammunition, water and stores to be supplied to his well-stretched divisions by a quicker route. The commanders of 150 Brigade box were well aware of this manoeuvre but could do little about it because of limited stocks of ammunition. There was a hope, however, that promised reinforcements in the form of an armoured column were on their way to assist the beleaguered Brigade.

On the evening of 28th May, at about 8.00 p.m. Dan observed the enemy over to the east, along his front. But it was quiet and they were at least half a mile away. However, at ten o'clock that night the Adjutant instructed Dan by phone that the Battalion was withdrawing and that he was responsible for clearing the area of three platoons of men, their equipment and ammunition. In the time given, with the few vehicles supplied, this seemed an impossible task. Greatly behind schedule, Dan's trucks moved off, dangerously overloaded with the goods of three platoons. Dan now had to march his men through the North Gap in the minefield to the new positions allocated to them. Because the men were dropping with tiredness, and to save time, he decided on a short cut. For guidance he relied upon the minefield tripwires, but realised too late that extra wires had been laid, he had followed the wrong ones and was lost.

Five minutes later, with not a landmark, I stood in blank, black desert, looking round me desperately. I dared not guess the direction to the North Gap, for there might be any amount of extra wire to mislead me. There might be arms of the minefield of which I was ignorant. I might be messing about with my platoon in the deadly light of dawn, in an evacuated area, in front of the enemy's guns and tanks. Already it was twenty past four. Dawn was at half-past five. "Oh God, oh God," I was saying to myself, "this is the worst thing I ever did."
My men were shuffling up quickly behind me, in the moon-darkness,

came the men gained a short respite, but no sooner had they settled for the night than the unthinkable happened to the dog-weary men; another move, another retreat. Hastily they packed up their weapons, water and personal gear, loaded up the trucks and joined the Company convoy. They sat on top of their baggage, moving back yet again to face their own longest day, not that they knew it at this point. The area held by 150 Brigade was reduced once more.

The Afrika Korps command realised that all would hinge on the events of the next day, 1st June. As soon as there was sufficient light, they began with a heavy aerial bombardment on the remnants of 150 Brigade's men, followed by intensive shelling. Dan's platoon had scarcely arrived at their fresh positions before the battle began. At first the guns of both sides fired over the hole in which Dan and some of his men were sheltering, swigging nervously from Major Huddleston's bottle of gin. Then they noticed that the Allied guns had ceased and the enemy had shortened his range and was shelling the slit trenches where the East Yorkshires were concealed.

Now the shelling became indescribably heavy. We knew in our hearts that such shelling could not be explained as shorts or overs. It was an aimed barrage. It shook our nerves, made our hearts thump, and gave us no rest. Right and left, before and behind, the air was incessantly split by explosions. The screaming cracking and rending of projectiles made one unbroken roar. We felt as if we had been tumbled into a basin and put out for the great birds to peck at.

Unable to move out of the pit he occupied, Dan could not understand what was happening until a row of tanks moving in single file was observed, in the distance, entering 150 Brigade's box. His fears were confirmed, this was not the relief armoured column but Rommel's tanks. Then the barrage stopped. They were being over-run by the enemy, tanks and armoured vehicles coming up on all sides. This was the real fight at last but they were clearly out-classed.

This is the way Dan described the final moments of the campaign in *The Trap*. At last he appears to be committed to action, even enjoying it.

Drake's Bren gun roared, chattered, snarled, bared her teeth in burst after burst, and was followed straight away by Herring's gun and King's. There they blazed from each angle of our position, all the fire I had, unleashed, set loose, invincible, screaming at our great enemies. God in Heaven, it was good to hear them. God it was good. Were we beaten, then? Were we broken? Had the tanks silenced us? Had they? By God, hear those guns, burst after burst after burst - hear the savage, incessant, intolerant chattering, chattering - hear them now, hear them - tanks, eh? tanks. Even tanks don't like it to rain lead - again, again, again, all three guns outbraying each other, hammering the air, with a combined roar like three pneumatic drills or all the riveting-machines in a shipyard. And the tanks answering with their wicked crackle - backwards and forwards lashed the storm of lead, while Phillimore fired regularly and steadily on a target behind us, and Bowers blazed off round after round from his anti-tank rifle.

We were transformed. The platoon was fighting. "We'll stop the buggers, sir, we'll stop 'em." We were taking lunatic risks, sticking our heads up into the torrent of lead that whipped about our pit. We laughed, infected by the monotonous iron laughter of the Brens.

Inevitably the ammunition for the Brens ran out, the other weapons the platoon possessed, although bravely and defiantly handled, were no match for the enemy tanks - in these last minutes the men threw grenades at the tanks, desperate to keep up a resistance, but it was useless. Dan realised that the approaching tanks, with just a little height advantage, would be able to shoot down into the pit in which he and his comrades were sheltering. Then the firing ceased and from the rim of his dug-out and with leaden heart Dan saw a platoon of British soldiers, hands in the air, moving towards the oncoming tanks. The battle was over.

I looked up, and found myself facing the German carrier, which was about forty yards away. Its Besa gun pointed square in my face ... "Kommen Sie her, Kamarad. You Kaput, for you the war is over."

9a. Jack Crossley, aged about nine, pictured with his new bicycle, or did it belong to his step-father? He would certainly have had trouble reaching the pedals. This is a photo he sent to Dan, who had been his school-teacher at Chiltern Street, after he and his family moved to Leeds.

9b. Dan pictured with a group of boys. They all four, including the teacher, seem to have a fair amount of the Huckleberry Finn element about them. Dan always said he preferred to spend time with his pupils rather than hobnobbing with the other staff. *(Picture: R. Bloomfield)*

9c. Summer holidays at Leven Canal. This jolly group shows Reg Bloomfield and Dan with their sisters enjoying a cup of tea on the riverbank. Joan and Eva are on the left, Reg's two sisters on the right. The houseboat "Mayhew" lies in the background. *(Picture: R. Bloomfield)*

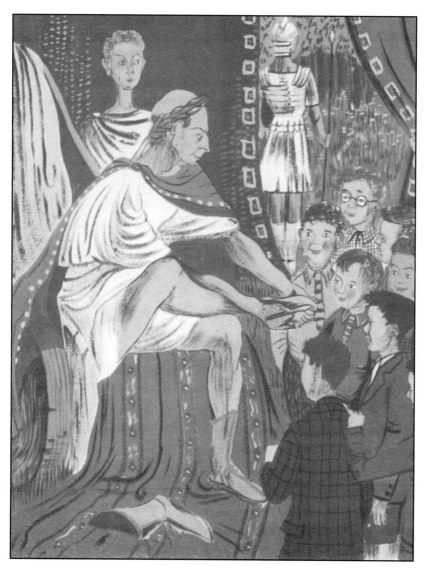

10. One of Joan Billany's nine illustrations for *The Magic Door*; the originals were destroyed when the house was bombed but she redrew them quickly and all agreed the second set were even better. The nine pictures, reproduced in bright colours, show the adventures of Mr Rocket's class who travel back in time. Here they watch with fascination as Julius Caesar cuts his toenails with a knife.

11a. Bonzo, a very important member of the Billany family. He and Elsie were buried under rubble the night in April 1941 when their home was bombed. He emerged unscathed, although rigid with fear, and stuck close to Joan throughout the following weeks, even spending a night in hospital with her. She said he saved her sanity.

11b. Harry and Elsie Billany with Bonzo in the garden of their Somerset home, taken during the summer of 1942. Although they appear relaxed and carefree here, they were both still recovering from severe injuries sustained in the bombing of Lakeside Grove.

12. David Dowie, Dan's friend, is on the extreme right of the group pictured here shortly after his escape from Dunkirk. His film-star good looks, seen in the single portrait, impressed Dan so much that he immediately decided that here was the ideal husband for his sister Joan. *(Picture: Imperial War Museum)*

13a. Two of Dan's sketches to illustrate the manuscript of *The Cage*. Both show life in the prisoner-of-war camp at Capua. Above, High Jinks in Hut 1, whose inmates described themselves as "round the bend" or "bag-happy".

13b. The Syndicate. This was a group of five prisoners formed for the purpose of sharing parcels of Red Cross food, which they cooked on improvised stoves. Reading from the left - Ted, Tony, Henry (sitting on the floor), David, and Dan. They are grouped round their stove drinking cocoa.

14. Dan's sketches of two prisoner-of-war camps. He describes the camp at Rezzanello as "a castle - very fake castle - with turrets and narrow stairs - a Folly." The one at Fontanellato was housed in an orphanage. Dan wrote home, "I've not told you much about this new camp. It is an ex-orphanage: immense staircases and hall, tons of marble, stained glass and windows too high for children to look out of."

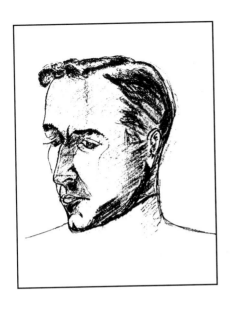

15. During his imprisonment Dan developed a talent for drawing portraits. Here are his pencil sketches of John Fleming above left, George Mathieson with his pipe and David Dowie. Dan could catch a likeness; compare this with David's photograph on the previous page.

16. One day the long-promised photographer arrived at Rezzanello to take pictures of the inmates. The Italians were anxious that the prisoners' families should see how well their loved ones were being cared for. David looks rather sullen but Dan took the opportunity to smile broadly to reassure his folks. These were the last pictures taken of the two friends.

Chapter 15

An earthly hell

Missing. Dan's family were devastated when the telegram arrived from the War Office. It stated baldly that Second Lieutenant D Billany of the 4th Battalion, East Yorkshire Regiment was officially posted as missing. What could they do? Only wait and hope. But for Dan, two o'clock on the 1st June 1942 marked the end of one extraordinary period of his life and the start of another.

> From the moment of my capture I had been in a condition like stupor. Things were not real to me. I was incapable of considering the loss of my platoon position as an incident in the larger battle. I had no thought of the future, I was quite careless of what happened to me ... 1 felt neither interest in, nor responsibility for, the future of my body.

The prisoners were rounded up, officers and men together and transported to a German encampment where Dan spent a cold night lying on the sand. He had no kit, no food, no water and could not locate any of his comrades. By the evening the officers were separated, driven west in lorries to the coastal village of Tmimi, where they were handed over to Italian guards. The camp here was a disgusting place. The sudden influx of hundreds of prisoners meant that the Italians had had no time to organise proper sanitary facilities and the air sang with swarming flies. But at least food was available, a small tin of bully beef and a biscuit for each man, and water was plentiful, although it was difficult to find anything in which to hold it. In desperation many men used their tin hats with the lining torn out. All through the day more British prisoners kept arriving, both officers and men. Some were in very bad physical condition from lack of food and especially water, suffering from the long march they had made from the battlefield.

The next move was to a prisoner-of-war camp at Syrte which was even worse. Dan described it as "an earthly hell". This was supposed to be a transit camp, yet some men spent up to five months there and many who entered never left. Nine thousand extra troops had recently been brought in from Tobruk which had fallen on 21st June and these wretched men were its vanquished defenders. They felt disgraced, let down, furious that Tobruk had been handed over so cheaply after all their efforts over so long a period. These swelled the numbers at Syrte.

In *The Trap*, Dan described the transfer of Allied prisoners over a period of five months, from one North African camp to another, all equally squalid and devoid of every amenity of civilisation. But in the main, officer prisoners spent little time in North Africa; they were usually transferred to POW camps in Italy quite quickly, either by sea or air. Dan himself was in Italy by the end of June 1942.

Although those officers who were transported by air were in a state of high anxiety all through the flight in case their aircraft attracted the attention of Allied fighter planes, their sufferings were considerably less than those of their comrades, sealed in the holds of the old German coffin-ships brought into use as prisoner carriers. Dan described embarking on such a journey.

I was taken on a small German merchantman at Tripoli, with about thirty other officers. At the quayside we saw five hundred British troops who had been captured with us, waiting to go on the same ship. They seemed, by the dust and sweat on them, to have marched some miles and they were very thin, ill and dirty. All were bearded. They wore the same shorts and shirts as they had on when captured six months before, but these were mostly in tatters. More than half the men were barefoot. A few who evidently had no clothing left at all, held a filthy blanket round them. Many were trembling with fever. Their thinness was such that their faces had lost individuality: all looked alike, and all like skulls. Cheek bones and jaws were prominent. Their eyes were large and bright, and stared out of their faces like the eyes of animals.

Although Dan did not personally experience transportation on a German POW vessel, he later had the chance to talk to fellow prisoners who had, and so could write movingly about the voyage. His accuracy in reporting has been corroborated by survivors. It was a nightmare journey. The men were shut down in the holds, in complete darkness during the hours of night. They were supplied with only the minimum of food and water and with no sanitary arrangements whatsoever. Many men who were unable to stand through illness or weakness lay on the bare steel floor in the swilling mess of urine, vomit, blood and faeces. Some of the fitter men used the ropes they found in the holds to rig up slings to support themselves above the stinking liquids on the floor. Once a day the prisoners were permitted to climb a ladder from the hold and spend ten minutes on deck, supposedly to empty their bowels over the ship's side but those in most need of fresh air were denied even this, being so weakened that they lacked the strength to mount the ladder, lost their grip and fell back into the filth below. At night the hatches were fastened down, leaving the men in the airless darkness. This also happened whenever there was an alarm which occurred maybe two or three times a day. No prisoners had been issued with life jackets but even if they had, the jackets would have been useless to the men in the battened-down holds.

The sea journey lasted about six days from embarkation in Tripoli to Naples, with a short call at Sicily and was prolonged due to the need to use a circuitous route. At Naples the prisoners were herded off the ship onto the quayside where another indignity awaited them. Photographers crowded round; their pictures were intended to bolster the morale of the Italians by showing the condition of British fighting troops.

In England the feelings of the Billany family and their friends swung between despair and hope. After all, "missing" is not the same as "killed", is it? Then, to their immense relief, the following telegram arrived on 26th June 1942.

OFFICIAL INFORMATION RECEIVED THAT SECOND LIEU-TENANT D BILLANY EAST YORKSHIRE REGT PREVIOUSLY REPORTED AS MISSING IS A PRISONER OF WAR STOP LETTER FOLLOWS SHORTLY STOP UNDER SECRETARY OF STATE FOR WAR.

Dan was safe, for the moment at any rate.

Chapter 16

Clickety Click - Camp 66

To Lieut. D_____,
British Prisoner of War,
Campo Prigionieri di Guerra No. 66,
Italy.

My Dear D_____,
    What a terrible shock it was for us all to hear you were Missing. Your poor Uncle ... It was a week of suspense ... Our relief when we heard you were a prisoner in Italy ... never so bad that they could not be worse, are they? So we must all make up our minds to make the best of it ... Your Uncle says ... most beautiful country, beautiful climate ... envies you your opportunity! ... must learn the language ... most beautiful ... See all those beautiful Cathedrals and Roman Ruins ... beautiful ... Regard it as a Heaven-sent opportunity rather than a ... Your Uncle has joined the _____ _____ _____. Last week we went to —— and saw ——. But Italy will soon ——. So keep your Pecker up, and think of the ——.

Your loving Aunt,
"_____"

David. Well, I see nothing to laugh at.
Dan. I was not laughing.

★★★

Dan was held initially at Camp 66, a huge prisoner-of-war camp at Capua about 20 miles north of Naples. It was situated on a wide area of flat ground at the foot of the Apennines and consisted of a number of compounds surrounded by a forest of barbed wire. At one time, there were 10,000 Allied prisoners held there. Although this was supposed to be a transit camp, and many prisoners were moved on after a week or so, such was the pressure of numbers that some were there for six months. Dan was in a seriously overcrowded compound, 70 yards square, which housed 150 officers living in a collection of tin-roofed wooden shacks. They wore the shirts, shorts and boots they had been captured in, and until parcels began to arrive from home, there was no prospect of any replacements.

    The problem was that the Italian authorities could not cope with such a huge influx of prisoners, following the Allied defeats in North Africa. Facilities were make-shift and primitive; the water supply failed regularly. The only food they could muster was acorn coffee, macaroni soup midday, and a roll of bread and a few dates or grapes for tea. Without the addition of Red Cross parcels, their prisoners would have starved; as it was, they steadily lost weight, became weak, run down and were always desperately hungry.

The shock and frustration of being held captive was intense and the only link with home was through the mail service. Prisoners were allowed to send a weekly letter and postcard and could receive any amount of mail, but the service was erratic and letters could take months to reach their destination. Dan's predicament was that he did not know where his family was. When he had last heard, his parents were about to move to Yeovil to join Joan but he had no address or point of contact. So his first letters were sent via his publishers and his Aunts' address in Hull. In them, his anxiety and worry about the family is mixed with his own frustration at being alone and adrift in a strange place without links to his former life.

Even in such crowded conditions, the first weeks of imprisonment were a lonely time. Each man felt isolated, suspicious of the others, jealously guarding his scraps of food, avoiding contact, relieved when at night he could draw a sheet over his face and feel more secure, because more alone. The bruising shame of capture, the sense of failure, and guilt about those comrades killed in battle took time to wear off. But gradually communication and trust were established, friendships were warily embarked on and social groups developed.

The syndicate system was the basis for these. Once Red Cross parcels started arriving in the camp, the men were grouped into fives for the purpose of sharing parcels, generally about three a week. They contained basic tinned rations, meat, vegetables, jam, cheese with sometimes a bar of soap, tea and chocolate. The men devised their own recipes and cooked up various concoctions on makeshift stoves fashioned out of mud and tin cans and fuelled with any wood or debris they could find. Maintaining these stoves and using the food to the best advantage became a full time job and one at which Dan worked wholeheartedly. The four others in his syndicate included two men who were to become his close friends during the months to come. One was David Dowie who figures later in the story; the other, George Mathieson, was the only man in the compound whom Dan had previously met. This was during the early period of capture in North Africa when for a few days they had shared a room in a hospital in Benghazi. Dan was suffering from dysentery and George was receiving treatment for a shrapnel wound in the elbow. But it was not until they met again in Capua that their friendship developed.

It was on 16th August, almost two months after his arrival at Camp 66, that Dan received his first mail from home. At last he had the family address - Pandean House, Peter Street, Yeovil; he was clearly delighted, even though he found it hard to picture the house and the family living there. His exuberant reply shows the intensity of his relief.

Dear Mother, Dad, Joan, Eva: Delighted! Have received letters from Dad (4th & 17th July) and Mrs Warner (23rd July) ... Dear me, the letters I didn't get in N.Africa! Stacks of 'em must be lost there. Mrs Warner says they sent me a cable - I never got it. No matter, this time I can't go wrong - I've got to stay put till Mail comes! It's grand to know my home address, and after all this time to see a letter that's actually come from home. What's Yeovil like? Have you had a nice summer? Is Joan still working? Must you find a smaller house? - I love the name of this one, and I'd like it big. Is Magic Door going to print? And do send me photos of yourselves and Pandean. How is your poor head, Mother? And Dad, is your leg improving at all? Joan, sorry to hear of your cold, hope well now. Hope "missing" report soon corrected - must have been awful shock. Love, Dan.

Dan's friend George Mathieson was a thirty-two year old lieutenant, who had worked before the war in the family business, a confectionery company called Clarnico. His background was opposite to Dan's in every way; he was from a wealthy family, public-school educated, mildly religious and as Dan says, "benevolently, devoutly middle-class". He was tolerant and easy-going, an intelligent man whose main interests were physics, mathematics and music. He and Dan played chess in the early days, but it was their mutual love of classical music that sealed the friendship. Later George managed to obtain a gramophone and they bought records through a helpful Italian contact and gave concerts to the other officers. George painstakingly copied out hymns from the single hymn book in the camp in preparation for the time when he would be able to form a choir.

Corporal Magione was the camp interpreter. He had been a Wagon-Lit attendant before the war and spoke good English. Dan described him as the true commander of the camp, "He had more ability, adaptability and energy than all his superiors". He made life easier for the inmates, at first by purchasing small items for them when he went into Capua, and later, as this service developed, by arranging to procure more ambitious objects, although for these they often had to wait until he visited Naples. Later they discovered his mark-up on the goods was inordinately high but at the time they were very grateful for what they could get. It was Magione who bought the gramophone and subsequent records, but he failed in his quest for a violin for George, who had a long frustrating wait until eventually he received the one which his Aunt Helen had sent from England.

Dan's first shopping list included a fountain pen and supply of notebooks, and before long he was absorbed in writing a new book. He says in his letter of 13th September 1942, "I'm doing rather a big job here which I've always wanted leisure for. I think it's going quite well," and from then on his letters contain periodic references to "my work", which is "the best I've done so far". Later he calls it his "big book", and on 7th November, he says that he is "on the last stretch, a grand feeling after 140,000 words." This was *The Trap* which, when it was published in 1950, was considered by many to be the finest book to come out of the war. Certainly Dan's confidence in what he was writing was not misplaced this time.

They say that a drowning man sees the whole of his life pass before his eyes in his last minutes. Dan, locked in this strange barbed-wire world where time seemed to be suspended, looked back into his life, and found there the basis for his new novel. It is the story of Lt. Michael Carr and his war experiences, which are closely based on those of Dan Billany. We have already quoted extensively from *The Trap* in those chapters describing Dan, the soldier. But it is much more than a vivid and beautifully written war memoir. The book begins with Michael Carr stationed at Helston, a huge army encampment in Cornwall in a period of relentless rain. He is in love with Elizabeth Pascoe and spends all his free time at the home she shares with her parents and teenage brother. This first part of the book is centred on the Pascoe family. Michael gets into their world through studying the family photograph album, and gradually their whole story is unfolded, from the engagement of the parents, (who he refers to as Mam and Dad), through years of hardship and failure up to the present time. The family he is describing is his own; the parents are his mother and father and Elizabeth is his favourite sister, Joan. He tells their story with compassion and love. It is very sad, in parts tragic, but it avoids the sentimental or sensational, and the end result is sincere and true. This was what he was writing during those first months at Capua at a time when he was missing his family so much. His recall of the early days in Hull is strong and vivid and setting it all down in *The Trap* was for him a way of being close to those who meant most to him.

Here are the last few lines of his letter of 6th September. Kit is Eva's baby who was only four months old when Dan left England.

Kit photos colossal - worlds better than any other baby photos married men have had sent - far more intelligent, advanced, lively, gleeful, bonny, exploratory. Have fixed both at head of my bed. Expression on one with Joan holding him is beyond words. Weather etc. splendid out here, but give me English wind and rain. Haven't seen a grey sky since I left. I long for one! I don't want eternal blue. How I long for England and home, and what a time I'll have when I come back! Remember me to Mrs Bloomfield. Love all, Dan.

Dan was meticulous in his weekly correspondence and kept a copy of his letters in a note-book. They were a marvel of compression and were numbered so that he could refer back and see to which letter or postcard his correspondent was replying; this was necessary because the mail was so erratic, some items arriving in weeks, others taking months. Each week a letter was sent to the family, but the postcards went to a whole range of people, usually in reply to letters from them. Thus he kept in touch with old friends such as Jack Crossley and Enid Mason, and more recently acquired ones like the Warners, all of whom wrote to him, Harry and Marjorie Smith from Mansfield, and George Richards, a schoolboy from Helston.

During September and October large numbers of other ranks arrived at Capua camp, many in appalling condition after imprisonment in the horrific desert camps followed by the sea journey to Italy. They were held in a separate compound but the Italian guards were generally sympathetic and meetings took place across the wire between officers and men who had been in their command. In this way Dan was able to talk to several members of his desert platoon and to send messages of reassurance to their families through the Billanys.

Dan and his fellow officers were held at Capua for five and a half months until the end of November. During that time conditions improved, but only slightly. The promised new compound never materialised; in fact space was even more restricted when a large tent was put up and forty Indian prisoners moved in. The bugs continued to multiply, watery macaroni soup was the only hot meal provided and mail trickled in frustratingly slowly. But Red Cross parcels from Canada became more plentiful and eventually individual parcels sent by the families began to get through. On 5th November, Dan's first one arrived and he was thrilled with the razor, toothbrush, face cloth and towel, basic clothing such as underwear, handkerchieves, sandals, shirt and pyjamas and a blanket which he acknowledged as "a Godsend". Books, chocolate, cigarettes came in a steady stream, and access to Italian goods and newspapers became routine.

It was not long before the men settled into a prison regime, friendship groups were formed and various activities established. By the middle of August, Dan was running an English literature and composition class and George was giving maths coaching. Everybody seemed to be involved in something. Learning Italian was quite popular; the Italian padre took the classes. David Dowie, another member of their syndicate took French and German lessons, and, as soon as the books arrived from home, settled down to teach himself sanitary engineering.

There were gramophone record concerts, performances by the drama group, revues, sketches, monologues. The so called Cloak and Dagger Brigade threw themselves into escape plans, but the only attempts made at Capua ended in disaster. There was bridge, solo whist, chess and Monopoly. Books were circulated, recommended, discussed; Dan gave lectures on *Wuthering Heights*, *King Lear* and Shakespeare's *Sonnets*. And sport flourished in various forms, although playing rugby on a baked earth pitch two yards wide and twenty long was far from ideal. David nevertheless persisted and seemed to enjoy it. Towards the end of their stay at Capua, walks in the surrounding countryside were introduced. A crocodile of men in threes, flanked by Italian guards would progress through the local lanes and villages and catch a glimpse of the country they were living in. One of their jokes was to walk so fast that the short-legged Italians had to run to keep up with them; another was to slip a daisy or sprig of fern into the muzzle of the ancient rifles carried by the guards. Dan kept a copy of a sad, emotional essay written by a Yugoslav prisoner which describes his feelings during one of these walks. This was probably a product of his composition class.

And Dan himself was in full creative flow. In letters home he wrote about his excitement in the progress of his new book. Interestingly enough, although people were aware that he was writing a book, he did not show it to anybody, nor did he tell them that he was a published author, with a children's novel about to come out, this being *The Magic Door*, whose publication was still being held up by the paper shortage. But they did get a chance to sample his talent in the comedy sketches he wrote and performed to great applause. And he was a popular contributor to the Camp 66 newspaper, the *Clickety-Click*.

Its editor was Lieutenant Roques who came from a journalistic background, but the writers included anyone who cared to submit copy. It came out every Monday afternoon and consisted of handwritten sheets of notepaper pasted onto an Italian newspaper and pinned up on the hut wall with barbs carefully untwisted from the barbed-wire fence. There was an up-to-date report on the war news, as culled from the Italian papers, a section of home news selected from letters from England, a strip cartoon, various comic features such as Mrs Unbeeton's "Cookery Nook", and a range of advertisements devised by George Mathieson. From the start *Clickety-Click* was a great success and appeared weekly from August to November; the first edition was on a single sheet of newspaper but eventually it ran to four or five. The main problem was obtaining the paste to gum the copy onto the backing paper. Lieutenant Roques' single pot of paste soon ran out and until Magione organised replacement stocks, various substitutes were tried such as golden syrup from a Red Cross parcel, nougat and hair cream. Dan was perceptive in realising that these copies of the *Clickety-Click* gave a unique insight into the life of the camp and the preoccupations of its prisoners. He collected the back numbers and stored them in a file which he took with him when they were moved on to another camp. But to his chagrin, the Italians confiscated it. He said bitterly, "We suppose all the stuff is now in Rome. If they read it they certainly won't return it."

Dan, with his love of food and inventiveness in recipe-making was the author of Mrs Unbeeton's cookery column. This was at a time when most of the real cooking was taking place on the make-shift mud stoves that the syndicates built to prepare the food from their Red Cross parcels. Although it was written in a very amusing style, it was also a practical guide as it included useful tips for making the stoves burn better and some excellent recipes given the availability of the ingredients. Biscuit porridge was a staple and cakes, the basis of which was soaked stale bread with the addition of raisins, jam, cocoa, or sugar depending on what was available, a luxury. He describes a favourite recipe in a letter written in early November. "Here is a breakfast dish I often serve to my syndicate: 1 tin bully, 10 apples (chopped), a few raisins. Cook in frying pan with plenty of curry! (Bloody good.)"

So life went on and it was not too unpleasant; there were lots of jokes, horseplay and comradeship. Apart from hunger and bugs and overcrowding, Dan seemed to be quite content and busily occupied . He was well-liked, looked up to as an authority on many subjects and had made some very good friends. In his letter of 13th November, he describes a typical day.

So here is the complete account I've promised so often of life at P.G. 66. At a quarter to eight in the morning George is getting out the breakfast things, Alec is folding his blankets, John is brushing his hair, and I am in bed. There is a shout, "Coffee" and everybody grabs a mug and dashes off to the coffee-dixie, from which an officer serves morning coffee. If it seems cold, I remain in bed. At eight o' clock an English-speaking Italian NCO comes in and shouts "roll-call". We assemble in three ranks: an Italian captain calls the roll. Then we cook our breakfast. Nowadays we have made another cooker, a portable tin one known as the "Hellbrew", and for the sake of getting all the food piping hot we often cook on both our old stove and the Hellbrew simultaneously, porridge and tea on one, ham roll and tomatoes, bacon, bully or what have you on the other. Then we eat: this is the best part of the morning. We finish breakfast usually soon after nine, and bullshit (= wash and polish) our pans. We are very proud of our syndicate pans, which we have bought in the last 2 months: 3 big saucepans (1 gall.) a mess-tin, and an excellent frying-pan. After this I wash and shave, read the paper, and do a spot of writing, if time. Or I read a canto or two of "The Faerie Queen." Then lunch is served at about 12 o'clock: macaroni or rice soup, meat or fish, vegetables. In the after-noon there may be a lecture ("Tibet", "Advertising", "Tiger-shooting", "Rare Books" etc.) or a walk. We prepare tea at 3.30, usually a big meal, apple pudding, creamed rice, pilchards, cheese, bread and jam, etc. Then I write some more, till dinner at 6: and after that we have tea, cocoa or hot milk, and I settle to a quiet, studious evening. What a life! Tons of love to you all, and Eva, Kit and Charles, Dan.

This version of events, written to reassure the family, vastly exaggerates the amount and quality of the food. For the true state of affairs, which describes, among other things, foraging among the dustbins for discarded cabbage stalks, you will have to read *The Cage*.

Two weeks later at the end of November 1942 came the move to a permanent camp. On the morning of departure, the men staggered to the station weighed down by the goods they had acquired in almost six months of captivity: books, records, music, cooking utensils, bars of soap (which they hoped to exchange for bread,) and food for the journey, saved from Red Cross parcels. The expected rations, "something in the nature of a sandwich", promised by the Italians never materialised and a Capuan Sandwich went into the prisoners' folklore as a syn-onym for nothing.

As the train clattered northwards through the night, Dan and his companions attempted to get some sleep, but it was almost impossible. They were packed too tightly into the compartment to allow for much rest; the blinds were kept down and the carriage had no lights. But the next morning a peep under the blind

117

revealed a new side to Italy. The air was chill, the landscape glittered with frost; during the night they had passed into the cold triangle bounded by the Alps, the Adriatic and the Apennines.

Chapter 17

Lontano - Camp 17

"Lontaaano, lontaaano," said the Italian padre and his long black beard waggled and his long white teeth showed. "Lontaaano, lontaaaano", the class repeated selfconsciously. The Italian padre sighed. He looked very sad. But he was a kind man so he only said, "No - that is not good. Italian is a very musical language and you must pronounce each syl-la-ble sep-ar-ate-ly. We will try again. Yes?" We took a deep breath and manoeuvred our tongues. It was all very trying. The batmen were preparing the mess; glasses and plates rattled; we wondered what was for lunch and doodled on writing-pads. Lontaano, lontaano. Far-away, far-away. Lontaano, the mountain looks blue, the bare little village, steep hill to the church, far-away, far-away. "La madre e il padre," said our padre very carefully and his eyes became gentle. Lontaano, Lontaano - blast the war, blast the war, lontaano la madre, lontaano il padre, lontaano, lontaano.

★★★

It was evening before the group reached their new camp at Rezzanello, in the mountains above Piacenza. It was dark, so they merely had a glimpse of an archway before being herded into the building. The next day they discovered that their prison was a gloomy, square-built, gothic castle with a turret on each corner.

The batmen had a story that it was built a hundred and fifty years ago by a Scotsman who married an Italian heiress, and certainly there was something dimly Scottish about it. It was like "Lucia di Lammermoor" - as Scottish, and as Italian. It was perhaps the scene-painter's impression of the stage manager's impression of Donnizetti's impression of Walter Scott's impression of the late seventeenth century; and the arch which led into the garden was faced with white marble as if the local funeral furnisher had been called in to finish the job.

It was set in romantically beautiful countryside, reminiscent of the Derbyshire hills through which Dan had cycled years earlier. On a fine day the Alps could be seen to the north. "... they are a marvellous sight," wrote Dan, "on clear mornings the snow shines with a rosy light high in the sky." Across those distant peaks lay Switzerland and freedom, but it all seemed just too far away.

They were amazed to find that at Rezzanello they were given real bedrooms furnished with cupboards, wardrobes and beds with spring mattresses and clean sheets. The higher ranks claimed the smaller and more exclusive rooms; mere second lieutenants, like Dan, were crammed up to fifteen to a room. Red Cross parcels were not handed out to the prisoners as at Capua, but centralised, so this meant the end of the syndicate system and cooking on mud stoves. This caused resentment at first. No longer were they able to divide the crumbs and lick out the tins; no longer did they have the choice of saving titbits for moments of direst need. Instead there was a cookhouse, manned by other ranks, who produced meals from the Italian rations supplemented by Red Cross parcels. Four meals a day were provided but they were meagre and went nowhere near satisfying the men. Breakfast was one biscuit and a cup of tea, except that sometimes they didn't get the biscuit.

The castle was cold, even colder than the frosty air outside and the walls gave off a damp chill. After the hot summer spent at Capua, where all they needed to wear was a pair of shorts, the constant cold depressed the prisoners and became a concern as serious as their gnawing hunger. Stoves were installed in the castle but there was no fuel and they sat useless, a tantalising sight to the shivering inmates. As usual, Dan played down the "damned cold" in his letters home, preferring to describe the wonderful landscape all around the castle. In an effort to keep warm, many men took a brisk walk round the garden or, like Dan, did a spot of energetic digging on the vegetable plot after lunch to work up a glow, then spent the afternoon in bed to conserve body heat. Escorted walks in the countryside were popular, but the drawback was the hearty appetites that the walkers worked up.

Eventually the men adjusted and took up the old routines of leisure activities and self-improvement. The gramophone and record collection had survived the journey from Camp 66 and were used for recitals in the common-room, the centre of activities. The promised violin from George's Aunt had still not arrived so he borrowed one from a batman and he and his pianist pal, Gervase (Cushy) Craddock, tucked themselves away in a side room to practise. Their efforts, audible throughout the building as a background to all other activities, were little appreciated. Christmas was only a couple of weeks away, and now George, with a complete set of hymn books, was ready to form his choir. From then on the walls echoed to the sound of carols sung to his three-part arrangements. Dan was an enthusiastic bass but his performance as a chorister left much to be desired. He was aware of his failings and preferred to practise in solitary confinement whenever possible, often in a remote lavatory.

The prisoners' spirits rose in anticipation as Christmas approached. At last wood had been delivered for the stoves. There was only enough for the evenings but they decided to save a little fuel every day so that the stoves could remain lit all Christmas Day. Strong rumours were circulating of extra Red Cross parcels, of a turkey obtained on the black market, and of a tin of condensed milk *each*.

George's choir gave of their best at the Christmas Eve concert; all the old favourite carols were sung, the audience joining in with the popular choruses. Dan wrote: "It was grand. I had the time of my life, boomed out the bottom Gs like Big Ben, and was rarely more than two tones flat." As for Christmas Day itself, all went wonderfully well, given the circumstances, and as the Senior British Officer said after dinner, it was a time they would all be glad to remember. Dan wrote to his family:

> ... more food than we could eat ... a big success. We went down periodically to eat, and then returned to our rooms, like gorged snakes, to digest what we had swallowed. ... Such was the quantity of food that I had to save my Christmas Cake and half the Pudding for the following day.

On New Year's Eve, a make-shift stage was rigged up and a concert given after dinner to mark the passing of 1942 and to welcome in 1943. It was a varied programme including a couple of Dan's comic verse monologues which were received with great applause, no doubt helped by the freely flowing red wine. In a particularly hilarious sketch he parodied the nightly routine of the Carabinieri, fully booted and spurred and wearing extraordinary hats, who tip-toed like hippotamus through the bedrooms checking every bed was occupied. Even the Italian interpreter was convulsed with laughter.

Amateur dramatics flourished in the camp and there were plenty of officers willing to take part, even to dress up to play the women. During the next few months there were several plays, concerts and music hall shows. Dan was recruited to play Dr Chasuble in *The Importance of Being Earnest*, a task he took very seriously, and by his account, it was a great success. And for other productions, he and David were always amongst the first to book their seats. Interest in lectures and lessons also increased. Everyone was either giving or attending classes or studying from books sent from home, frequently all three. Dan and David were working on French and had started German and Italian. Influenced by the beauty of his surroundings, Dan took up sketching quite soon after the move to Rezzanello. Even when it was too cold to study or write he persevered with his drawing. His first attempts were to capture the wonderful views from the castle windows, but later he turned his hand to portraits. Dan was pleased with the results, as were his sitters, and he gained quite a reputation with his likenesses. As usual, he took this hobby very seriously and wrote to his sister about his work.

> I'd like to show you them, Joan, you could tell me a lot about the application of masses of shade. You know my preoccupation with detailed accuracy. I think you would approve of the care and integrity of my drawing, though you would find plenty to criticise in my technique.

One day a photographer, introduced by the Italians as a propaganda exercise under the guise of a concession, arrived at Rezzanello, laden down with his equipment. There was a mad scramble to get a decent shave, borrow a tie and put on a big smile, all to deceive the folks at home into thinking that Camp 17 was more like a holiday camp than a prison. Dan's photograph shows a grin as wide as ever and he holds a cigarette with a graceful air, but there was no way he could disguise his thin cheeks and receding hair.

News of the progress of the war was of vital importance. The prisoners in Camp 17 had two sources to choose from. The Italian newspapers' version was translated by Jock, a fluent linguist, but this was obviously heavily biased in favour of the enemy. It contrasted with the other source, information passed by the Italian doctor to his British counterpart in the strictest confidence; this was almost certainly news given out in BBC broadcasts. In this way they heard about Montgomery's triumph at Tripoli and the Russians' steady advance westwards. Dan and his father discussed the war in their letters by means of a code to fool the censor. Rather obscure references to Uncle Joe and Old Hatchitts pepper their correspondence, but these were comments rather than the passing of information as letters often took months to arrive.

And the war was reaching even closer to the camp at Rezzanello. Night after night the castle's shutters rattled to the sound of bombing raids, which the prisoners rightly interpreted as RAF attacks on the cities of northern Italy, usually Turin. It was comforting to think of their fellow-countrymen so close and so active.

Dan constantly fretted about the family back home; he worried about their health and regularly implored them to take plenty of rest and look after themselves. None of the Billanys had recovered completely from the physical effects of the bombing - Harry never would. Elsie's head wound was still causing concern; she was under the care of a consultant with an operation looming up. Even Joan, who had got off the lightest, was suffering with recurring ear trouble.

Dan had been dragged away from his family just when they had need of him most and landed up in Italy, a frustrated bystander whose only contact was by mail, imagining his parents and sister struggling in a strange house in new surroundings, to which he could not relate. Dan's family was vitally important to him, he wanted to feel that he was needed, especially by Joan, the kid sister he had always protected. Of necessity, Joan had struck out on her own by moving to Yeovil, where she had rented a house big enough for her parents to move in with her. But Pandean House, despite its fancy name and big rooms was uncomfortable and badly infested with mice, so Joan had scouted around and found Newlands which Dan thought had "a fine bourgeois sound about it". He learnt of their move in early February 1943 and immediately pressed for a detailed description of the place. He felt a desperate need to be able to visualise the home to which he hoped he would soon be returning, to "settle down and live happily ever after".

Harry suffered from a heart condition, a legacy of his tuberculosis and injuries received in the bombing, but he was not the sort of man to sit down and rest all day, in spite of Dan's urgings. He liked to potter around the house and garden and increasingly his time was taken up acting as a long-distance secretary to Dan

- acknowledging letters on his son's behalf; sorting out his finances; passing information on to relatives of other prisoners-of-war; and he was in regular contact with Nelsons concerning the publication of *The Magic Door*, delayed yet again because of the wartime paper shortage. All these were jobs he enjoyed; they made him feel useful and writing came easily to him. He even tried his hand at short story writing and sent some examples to Rezzanello for Dan's opinion.

Dan was working hard on his own project, his war novel, *The Trap*, now undergoing final revision. Everyone knew Dan Billany was writing a book. Within the camp it was difficult to keep anything secret, given the crowded conditions in which they all lived, but Dan kept remarkably quiet about it. He did ask David to read some of the early chapters, but no-one else was shown the manuscript.

★★★

Much of *The Trap* is a direct retelling of Dan's life. His family, his schooldays, the bombing of his home, and his experiences as a soldier are all included. And on this base the novel is built, with the addition of fictional characters, relationships and turns of plot.

Dan was right, it was his best work so far. By now words came to him easily, and his descriptions were masterful.

Bonzo stirred, stretched, pushing his forepaws forward and pressing his jaw down between his forelegs: then he went out, and I glimpsed him earnestly trotting about the lawn. Beyond and above the peaceful garden thus framed in a rectangle of window brooded the vast clear sky, paling from liquid fire at the horizon to pale night-blue tinged with amber at the top of the window. Three little horizontal clouds, floating above the sun like slivers of wood laid to dry over a fire, caught all the golden light, and shone out from the shining sky a hundred times brighter: as if the sky were a smooth backcloth with a dazzling lamp behind, and the canvas had frayed along the folds in three places, letting the light through. The long beams of sunset fell redly on the dust which flecked the window outside, and drew in shadows a tangle of sweet-pea tendrils on the glass. Then Mother drew the other half of the black-out curtains, and war had shut out the evening.

It is a story told from a personal standpoint, into which Dan pours his feelings about the war and his whole view of life. Above all, there is a great love and sympathy for humankind. He is as concerned about the lives of the Egyptian peasants glimpsed from the troop train as he is about the destruction of a simple family whose home is blitzed in front of them. His political convictions pervade the novel. The Pascoe family struggling against poverty, ill-health, and the class system is painted with great sympathy, especially the mother who, tight-lipped, faces all that life can throw at her unflinching. And they succeed after all their set-backs in making a reasonable life for themselves - until the bomb which destroys it all. The author frequently breaks into the narrative to speak directly to the reader. This follows a digression on the working class.

> Oh yes, yes, yes, yes! I know I'm holding up the story, and I don't care a damn. I've wanted to say this for years. Rancorous? By God I'm Rancorous. I'd be ashamed to the very depths of my soul if I could write about my class without heat.

The book is primarily a war story. Lieutenant Michael Carr's involvement with the Pascoes is through his love affair with their daughter Elizabeth, and the next section of the novel is written in letters exchanged between the two of them when Michael is posted to a new base at Pwllheli. Increasingly the men in his command play a more important role in the novel. Michael feels a much closer affinity to them than to his fellow officers, for the most part middle-class toffs leading superficial, self-centred lives. In contrast, Private Shaw is a working class boy who has never had a chance, a dishonest, immature lad who faces the world with anger and bravado. Michael's handling of Shaw and the other men in his platoon is central to the story and these relationships are developed throughout the third part of the book, which covers the journey to Egypt and then across the desert to the front line at Gazala. The battle itself is described in frightening detail, concentrating on the men's reactions and support of each other, told in human terms rather than military ones. The Germans hardly figure in it all except as machines or noises off. Throughout, Michael is much more critical of the mismanagement of the army and the war in general than he is of the enemy. It is significant that the only serious injury he describes is that of Corporal Willis who accidentally shoots himself through the leg.

The Trap is a realistic portrayal of war, owing nothing to the popular convention of the time: adventures featuring brave officers, loyal batmen and deeds of daring escapades. Dan Billany combines in this book a range of elements, the love story, the family shattered and dispersed by war, the carnage of the battlefield, and the relationships of the men sharing that experience. Together they form an integrated whole, a compelling, moving story, punctuated by Dan Billany's own voice.

Here is his comment on a theme that recurs throughout his work, his regret at the loss of childhood.

> Have time to remember the child you were, give him a deep thought now and then, be sensitive to all you can of the past, and it will reward you with bright shoots of everlastingness. To live in the present moment is easy, any animal does it: to live in eternity is really to live.

The Present is a room; the Past furnishes it, the Future lights it.

The Trap has additional impetus because it was written only months after the experiences which form the climax of the book. No wonder the reader can feel he is right there, a part of the action. No wonder that Dan was so excited about his work that he constantly mentioned it in his letters home. He finished the first draft shortly after the move to Rezzanello and then came the process of revising and copying it in neat black ink script into a series of Italian exercise books. This took another five months and finally the finished stack of nine books was carefully wrapped and hidden in a Red Cross cardboard box under his bed.

★★★

By the early part of 1943 things had settled into a far from unpleasant routine at Camp 17. One could almost describe it as cosy, now that the stoves were burning regularly and the chill of the stone castle had abated. Warm friendships were developing too. Dan was very comfortable with the group of men who were based at the end of his dormitory. These included George Mathieson, although he was always a bit of a loner, and since coming to Rezzanello was devoting more and more of his time to music, spending many hours in practice with Cushy Craddock. Also in the gang were John Mills, John Fleming and Alec Harding. They had been in prison together for nearly eighteen months, and by this time knew each other very well. However, Dan's closest friend was another lieutenant, a member of his original syndicate at Capua, David Dowie.

David Arthur Dowie was only twenty-three when he was captured but had by that time already had a pretty distinguished war record. He had served with The Royal Northumberland Fusiliers in France and had been rescued from the beach at Dunkirk. Later he was posted to North Africa where he had been in the thick of some horrific fighting, one of the worst moments being when his wounded signaller died in his arms. He had been captured at Tobruk and thence transported to Italy by the same route as Dan. His background was similar to Dan's in that he came from a working class family and was in the process of making his way in the world through education. David, the youngest of nine children, grew up in south east London. His father had died in 1936 and his mother, who was not in good health, looked to her children to support her. David entered Local Government when he left school and worked diligently at night classes to gain the qualifications he needed to make his way in the Town Planning department. He would really have liked to have been an architect but that seemed an impossible goal.

In other respects he was the opposite of Dan. He was strong and graceful, an athlete who excelled at all sports; he was uncomplicated, confident, at ease with himself and in charge of his own life. He was engaged to be married to just the right sort of girl, to whom he wrote every week. The other men in the camp saw Dan and David's friendship as a union of opposites, David the extrovert - relaxed and simple, Dan the intellectual - nervy, introverted and intense. But the two shared the same opinions, valued the same qualities and each respected the other very highly. Their relationship intensified so that towards the end of their imprisonment they were often the butt of ribald comments from the other prisoners. This would be at their next camp, Fontenellato, when they were working together on *The Cage* and never seemed to be out of each other's company.

But at Rezzanello, their relationship was just developing. There is no doubt that Dan admired David for all the qualities he himself did not possess. But he was also attracted by his physical appearance. In typical Dan-style, the more he thought about it, the deeper he became involved, and before too long, thoughts of David obsessed him and he was in love. At first he didn't admit it even to himself. Instead he decided that David should marry his sister. He wrote a postcard to Joan, in his usual compressed script, telling her of this plan in January 1943.

> Dear Joan: I have to write you on an important matter affecting your future - have decided you should marry David Dowie. (pause for reflection). Do not therefore, (unless you must!) marry Gaumont-British, or any local Flying Officers. David is, on my recommendation, the right and only husband for you. He is 23, very attractive, intelligent, generous, and in every possible way nice. However he is already slightly engaged, but this may not be an insuperable difficulty. You see how I think of you! (I'm not entirely haywire in this matter.) You'd like him: have shown him yr. photos. Love Dan.

And it seems he really was serious, in spite of the fact that David had a fiancee and Joan a steady boyfriend, for he repeated it all in a letter the following week just in case the postcard did not arrive. Some weeks later, when he heard that Joan had finished with her boyfriend, Ken, Dan wrote in great detail outlining the type of man she should be seeking for a husband.

> ... good-looking, physically charming & strong, a graceful mover - dancing, swimming, sport. He must have a sense of justice, and a native contempt for traditions merely as such. Must have our kind of unserious attitude towards religion & the other bogeys: kind, merry, truthful, self-knowing, self-respecting, absolutely courageous: must look you in the eyes, and be able to understand the thoughts which may underlie your words - and answer rightly, not just superficial gab.

This of course was a description of David Dowie, at least, as Dan saw him.

David was becoming understandably nervous about Dan's efforts to get closer to him, and when Dan, who couldn't help himself, eventually declared his love, David was shocked, embarrassed and as a result shunned his company. It seems that, throughout his life, Dan had a compulsion to reveal his feelings. He was unable like most of us to have secrets and private thoughts; they had to be expressed, if not verbally, then in writing. Perhaps this is what marks the writer off from the rest of society. Certainly, Dan maintained that in all his work, including fiction, his aim was to express the truth. However the result of this self-revelation was a rift between the two friends. Dan was working on his revision of *The Trap* and channelled all his energies into this; David pursued his studies assiduously - shorthand, engineering and building construction, and joined in the social life of the camp, playing bridge, going for walks, involving himself in all the sporting activities.

But Dan was not one to give in. He usually got what he wanted and he was determined about this. He wrote a poem for David, which seems to have done the trick because soon after, their friendship was back on the old footing. This is it, including the bracketed comment at the end.

"You hurt my hand with wringing, let us part
And cease this idle theme, this bootless chat
Withdraw your siege from my unyielding heart
To love's alarms it will not ope the gate.
   Dismiss your vows, your feigned tears, your flattery,
   For when a heart is hard they make no battery."

You order where your statutes do not stand.
Some servants and some soldiers draw no pay
And are not correspondent to command,
Nor come when called, nor go when sent away:
   Canute, for all his circumstance and pride
   Made precious small impression on the tide.

"Dismiss my vows" - dismiss, you mean, my love -
With pleasure, and dismiss my features too,
And all other properties remove
Which share the grave offence of loving you,
   Dismiss my arms and legs and heart and brain
   And uncreate my self and start again.

When nature carved my limbs, was I consulted?
Do I control the movement of my blood?
Could I reject that nose so oft insulted?
(An organ I would barter if I could)
   Just so, I can't be cancelled by degree
   And love not you because you love not me.

Whatever you may think or say or do,
I love you and will love you till I die,
And those are facts which don't depend on you

And which I cannot alter if I try.
You say your heart is hard and will not yield -
So much the worse, since there my love is sealed.

So why not make the best of the position?
Let's lay our self-protective armour by,
There's common kindness in our disposition
And common sense and plain humanity
For God's sake let's be easy as before,
And trust each other and be sane once more.

(If you see what I mean, like.)

Dan wrote the poem on the inside cover of Volume One of the manuscript of
The Trap. He offered the book to David, ostensibly for him to read the story, but
really he wanted to give him the poem. The first stanza, in inverted commas,
expresses David's resistance; the rest of the poem is Dan's avowal that he cannot
change his feelings. But there is a compromise in the final couplet, "... let's be
easy as before, and trust each other ..." And the bracketed comment at the end
serves to put it all on a lighter, more personal level. Years later, after the war,
when Harry typed up the poem, he used this line, "If you see what I mean, like",
as the title. It seems reasonable to assume that when their friendship resumed,
they were no more than just friends. David was firm in his rejection of a sexual
affair and even Dan, although undoubtedly homosexual, accepted the censure of
the times against what were usually referred to as 'unnatural practices'. Added
to which, a terribly overcrowded prison camp offered no privacy night or day.

The world outside the prison camp seemed very far away and Dan, like thousands of others, found it hard to imagine how he was going to pick up the threads
after the war. He wrote to Eva, in the spring of 1943, that he had been the slow-
est of the family to grow up but had now pulled his ideas into shape.

Sometimes I try to work out what life is going to be like after the war, but
it's very hard to see reality from a prison camp. Certainly the old days of
Lakeside are gone and we shall have to find something bold to put in their
place. I'm determined not to let my life dribble away as it did before - I
shall go back at first to teaching, I daresay, but I mean quite definitely to
earn money by writing and not to be dependent on any job. And I am
resolved to marry ...

At the beginning of April the whole group was on the move again; but it was
only a short journey this time, from a castle to an orphanage.

Chapter 18

Orphans - Camp 49

Camp 49 was in Fontanellato, a village ten miles north west of Parma on the Lombardy plain. Initially the move was unpopular with the group of men who had shaken down into a familiar, comfortable pattern of work and leisure activities at Rezzanello.

The change to Fontanellato was at first completely disruptive. For a fortnight we wandered unhappily about the corridors, feeling that there was no place safe from disturbance and nothing to do even if we found such a place ... We were in the no-man's-land of life, a kind of purgatory of aimlessness. To say that we were unhappy hardly describes it. We were without a reason for waking, eating and moving.

The orphanage at Fontanellato had only recently been completed. It was intended as a home for girls, financed by money from pilgrims to the shrine of Madonna Del Rosario which stood next door and was tended by a closed order of nuns. Instead of young girls, the first orphans were six hundred and fifty Allied POWs, officers, batmen and cooks who moved into the place in batches in the spring of 1943. Camp 49 was an imposing block of a building, four storeys and a basement, in the shape of a letter 'E'. The two outer wings were dormitories whilst the inner one was the hall. An elaborate facade covered the entire front, arcading providing a covered walk-way at ground floor level, with a balcony above accessible from the first floor. The double doors at the centre, with pillars each side, were surmounted by a series of classical features. Internally the place was as pretentious as the outside. Once through the ornate doors, an impressive marble staircase swept up from the main hall to a balcony which ran round three sides of it. The section over the front door, which overlooked the main street of the village, was the long bar where there was a daily issue of wine - a choice of Chianti, Vermouth or Marsala. The windows here provided an observation point for officers to ogle the local girls strolling by on their way to the cemetery. In the central hall, the mosaic floor reflected the multi-coloured light flickering through tall stained-glass windows, which were decorated with uplifting Biblical scenes deemed suitable for orphan girls. In spite of its massive appearance and grandiose features, the orphanage was shoddily built and unstable; when a few men skipped on an upper floor the whole place shook.

But after the deprivations of earlier camps, conditions were luxurious. The dormitories were equipped with spring mattresses and bedside cupboards; there were lavatories (albeit squatter-type, child sized) and washbasins on every floor,

ant way to pass an evening, listening to the popular tunes of the day, singing along and, after a few glasses of the rough red vino, larking about dancing with each other, pretending to waltz sedately or galloping up and down the room in the Gay Gordons. Sometimes there were concerts of a more serious nature when George would play Beethoven and Pat Gibson would sing Schubert. Dan enjoyed these equally as much.

Stuart Hood listed three categories of prisoner at Fontanellato in his book *Pebbles From My Skull*. The first settled easily into camp activities, the lectures, sports and entertainments seen as a sort of extension of prep school. Neither Dan nor David had been anywhere near a prep school but they fitted into this group. The second were the escapers, single-minded in their determination to get out, however futile this might be. And the third were the rebels, refusing to involve themselves in any activity, sullenly and angrily sitting out their imprisonment. And there were a few outside any category who had no resources for dealing with the situation and had to be watched in case they threw themselves at the wire and were shot to pieces.

Perhaps this is the point to say something about the would-be escapers, known as the Cloak and Dagger Brigade. The 'trench in the sports field' escape was not the only attempt. It was considered to be virtually impossible to get out of Camp 49 because it was a single building. Nevertheless there were those who tried. The only way to tunnel was to start in the basement and this was attempted but it was very hard work, and not long before the tunnel was discovered. Subsequent plans were thwarted by the Italians digging a trench or moat round the perimeter of the camp and conducting regular searches of the basement. Tony Davies and a number of pals continued to dig however, excavating a cavity under the short flight of stone steps which went up to the front doors. Toby Graham and Eric Newby joined the team chipping away at concrete with improvised tools and making very slow progress. Their aim was to make a bolt hole where a small number of them could hide if and when the Germans arrived to take over the camp. The hole was never finished and as it happened never needed. But it allowed these frustrated captives to feel that they were doing something positive; digging had almost become a therapy.

For the majority of prisoners, entertainments and activities continued to be popular. The Rezzanello men gave another performance of *The Importance of Being Earnest*, less well received this time. Dan was still in demand for his recitations of comic doggerel verse. He was beginning to find this rather a chore but was obviously successful as he wrote home, "my rhymes at our last show brought the house down". On the more serious side, he continued his study of psychology, pestering his father for more books on the subject, and he worked hard at art, now engrossed in life-drawing classes, given by an architect newly arrived at the camp. Art was a popular activity among the prisoners, and oil paints and drawing materials were among the goods on sale in the canteen. Perhaps they were inspired by the spectacular views from the top floor of the orphanage from

132

which one could see across the flat farmlands of the Po valley to the distant mountains, the Dolomites, and Switzerland. Others painted the view of the village from the front of the building and there were portraits too. The best work was displayed at camp art exhibitions; Dan was a regular contributor. Again he asked for Joan's advice and wrote to her: "In accordance with your instructions I have spat on all my pictures. It makes the ink run. Should I try peeing on 'em?"

News came from Joan that at last *The Magic Door* was ready for publication. She was handling business matters instead of her father who was suffering from a bout of depressive illness. Dan was delighted by the news of his book, especially as he hoped to follow up its success with *The Trap*, which was almost finished.

Now he began to look around for another project. At this time, the friendship between Dan and David was so close that collaboration seemed the answer. It gave them a common project to work on, ideal for Dan as it inevitably meant that he and David were drawn even closer, and it must have been a fascinating experience for the younger man to write a book with a real author. They decided to write the story of their imprisonment, from arrival at Capua right through to the present. They began work in May 1943. By this time they were distanced enough from the early part of their captivity to look back at it objectively, and they had a lot of material to hand, such as David's diaries, Dan's notebooks and the copies of his letters home. Moreover, they were surrounded by a host of interesting characters, who seemed ready made for inclusion in the story.

★★★

Their book, originally entitled *For You the War is Over*, but which was eventually published as *The Cage*, reads like a factual account of their life in prison but it is fictionalised to the extent that names have been changed and incidents altered for dramatic purposes. Their methods of working varied. Sometimes each wrote separately, but more often they sat down at a table, one or other with the pen, and composed together. In the evenings they would read over what they had written, and other prisoners would be invited to comment; some even contributed - George certainly did. (He plays a major role in the story as the violin-playing mathematician, Henry). Taking into account the conditions under which they had to work, the wonder is that the book succeeds as a whole, but it does. Some of the more amusing and psychological elements of the story can be attributed with certainty to Dan; David's contribution is simple narrative and recollection; descriptions of chains of events. He wrote as he was, straightforward and direct. Dan realised that David had no inarticulate blaze inside him, demanding to be noticed. For Dan it was different. He was the driving force behind the collaboration and also was striving to express what he described as "the crying need within me".

It's a bloody good job David and I are working on this together, because the clear antithesis of our writing will make the book, and may make me - may let me see myself and, at last, write what I want to write.

The Cage opens with a letter, the one quoted at the beginning of our Chapter 16. It is more than likely it was based on a real letter (selections of prisoners' mail from home were often displayed at Camp 66, as items of general news and interest). In it, some fellow's aunt urges him to look on the bright side - to make the most of time spent in such a beautiful, interesting country as Italy. This leads into an account of life at Capua, in the baked earth compound where the only view was that of barbed wire.

From the start, the authors establish their reasons for writing now, whilst it was all still happening.

This book is intended to take you into the strange world where we have now been living for a year ... If we delayed writing till we got back to England we should gain in tranquillity, but in everything else we should lose ...

Dan and David were determined to be totally open and to write without reserve. Many other soldiers went on to publish war and POW memoirs, but *The Cage* is exceptional in the honest way in which it treats relationships, including their own.

The book divides naturally into three parts. The first which describes life in Camp 66 at Capua, gives an impression of day to day life, the hardships, the hunger, the deprivations and the agony of physical adjustment to prison. But it is not without humour. The narrative varies from short snatches of dialogue to descriptions, instructions, recipes, jokes and lengthy conversations. Rumours abounded and any that was considered "both new and feasible" was announced by the Rumour Bell, a stainless steel dixie which was struck like a gong.

Bong!
Carry on.
Canadian Red Cross parcels tomorrow: that's *definite.*
Oh Boy!
One *Pound* of *Butter!*
One *Pound* of jam!
One tin of *Bully!*
A bloody great packet of bloody great biscuits!

Food is a constant preoccupation and source of fantasy. (El Capitano was the name they gave to the Italian officer in charge of messing.)

"Dining at El Capitano's this evening - their macaroni soup is so delicious - I was privileged to catch a glimpse of the distinguished big-game hunter, Captain Mohawk, wearing the simple but stylish trousers which he has done so much to popularise. The secret of the garment - I am permitted to whisper it - is that the Captain wears the garment with the fly to the rear, and - as all the buttons have become detached - fastens them at a strategic point with an ordinary safety-pin, as a precaution ..."

Even dramatic events like the death of two escapers, or the visit of the Swiss Red Cross representative, although sympathetically treated, contain a vein of humour.

Early in the story we are introduced to the main characters, members of Dan and David's syndicate who were all captured in North Africa in the summer of 1942. They are real people but, apart from the two authors, their names have been changed. Like a cast list in a theatre programme, their backgrounds and personalities are given a brief mention and later developed by such devices as eavesdropping on their day-dreams, their discussions and arguments.

For dramatic emphasis, Dan and David deliberately contrast the serious passages of introspection and the reliving of painful memories with scenes of almost Goon-like humour and slap-stick. Many of the young inmates of Capua had joined the army straight from public school or university and the desperate jollity of their horseplay reveals their immaturity. The wilder inhabitants of Hut 1 described themselves as "Round the Bend" or "Bag-Happy"; it was the home of make-believe. When the lights went out at ten thirty, the fun began on the signal of a whistle, and the command, "Night work on the tunnel will now begin". At this the officers started thumping their bed-trestles rhythmically on the floor and making hissing sounds and hydraulic noises with their mouths. It was like being in a foundry. The Italian sentries gaped in amazement and shook their heads sadly, "The mad English", they muttered.

In contrast, the homesickness and sadness from which they all suffered come over well in the account of an Italian lesson when the padre is trying to teach them to say "lontano", meaning "far away". This has already been quoted this as an introduction to Chapter 17.

From its inception, Dan and David intended to illustrate *The Cage* themselves. But they were neither of them experts and Dan wrote to Joan that he was relying on her to tidy up the pictures before the book went to press. The manuscript, now deposited at the Imperial War Museum, contains pen-and-ink sketches inserted into the narrative at appropriate places. "Group of Liberal Peers about to enter the House" shows a queue of men patiently waiting to visit the latrines. "Mohawk, Kittyhawk and – hawk" illustrates three shaven-headed prisoners, the third nickname, too rude to print, refers to Dan. This is the description of how he had his head shaved.

At last he made up his mind. He went to the Italian Barber, passed his hands over his (own) head and said "Tutti - tutto - tutte," confident that one of them, if not all, would convey his meaning. The barber smiled and took up his clippers. Dan sat down on the stool outside Hut 2, and the barber began to expose to the Italian sunshine areas which had been concealed for more than a quarter of a century ...We met Dan in the doorway of the hut; he ducked, sidled past, avoiding our eyes, and looked in a mirror. He tried to smile at his reflection, but under that dome the smiles looked incongruous, irreverent. Fear dawned in his eyes. "What have I done?" The naked head was an egg, a bladder.

Spirits fall as time passes, conditions worsen and there is still no sign of any of the rumours being true. The progression of the seasons is not mentioned, but shortly before Christmas, six months after their arrival, the men of Huts 1, 2 and 3 prepare to leave for a permanent camp. This is how Dan and David describe their last view of Camp 66.

We leave Capua to Time and Silence and two Americans. And Capua has started to forget us. Just as the world will forget the sorrowful madness of this war, the wires will be taken down from the fences and the compounds ploughed back into the fields. Peasants will bring the corn in from where we cooked breakfasts, read letters, and lived our life of rumours. There will be harmless gossip in the evenings in the place where M—— was shot whilst trying to escape, close by the road he never reached.

Good-bye, Capua, for ever. Your silence is the fulfilment of a rumour. The birds have gone to another cage. Your silence, Capua, is what we shall remember of you. As the train carries us north, we know that inside the fence which edged our world for six months is peace at last - if both the Americans are asleep. Peace: stillness: the impersonal floodlights: the stars: the faintly moaning sentries: and regularly at its inevitable intervals, the sound of No. 5 latrine flushing itself hopelessly all night.

The rest of the book, which describes life at Rezzanello and Fontanellato, Camps 17 and 49, develops in a different style. The jokes, the camaraderie and the fun are played down and the book takes a serious turn examining the psychology of the prisoners, how they variously cope with their situation, and how they handle the friendships and tensions which develop between them. The focus of this part of the story is that of one young officer's love for another and is based on the development of Dan and David's own friendship. It is presented in a fictional form as the conflict between Alan Matsen (an invented character) and David Dowie (himself).

Alan Matsen is not a very attractive character. He is an unhappy man, ill at ease with himself, immature and lacking in confidence. He sees in David all the qualities he wished he possessed and develops a school-boy crush on his hero. He waits long-faced at corners, hoping David will speak to him; he leans over the railing of the top floor balcony at the orphanage, miserably looking down on the foreshortened figure of David playing bridge in the hall below. And, as he becomes bolder, he approaches his idol offering him gifts, begging for his time, his conversation and eventually his affection. David is irritated and embarrassed by his attentions and discusses with Dan how he can distance himself without

136

being too cruel. Other characters also are drawn in and comment on the relationship, but Dan is the one who is most involved and gives sensible advice to both parties. This is the mature, reasonable side of Dan, the one who was studying psychology and enjoyed looking for motives and reactions.

But in the person of Alan, we see the other side of Dan, the insecure introvert, desperate for love. The fictional relationship is undoubtedly a retelling of the problems the authors themselves experienced in the development of their own friendship. True, Alan is so spineless that it is hard to see Dan in him at all, but this is just one aspect of his character. In this part of the book, he has split himself in two: the confident, rational, side observing and commenting on the problem; and in contrast the utterly hopeless, despairing side that cannot go on living unless David accepts him and his love. Here is a typical piece of dialogue.

Alan. It hurts, no use pretending it doesn't. You see, it's different, I know, from your viewpoint, but to me - well, neither Henry nor anybody else here would give up his life for you. You see ...?

David. But nobody asked *you* to, Alan. It would be just another gift you force on me - one that's worth more to you than to me.

Alan. It's pretty hard.

David. Only because you make it hard. Why don't you accept the facts. Stop torturing yourself and stop irritating me.

Alan. Because I can't. No, it's no use saying what isn't true. I can't stop liking you. I can't. I can't remake myself. It isn't in my power.

David. Then you'll have to take what's coming to you, and take it without whining. The whole of this tie-up between us comes from your side. I don't seek you, and I don't want you. It's absolutely one-sided. You can't hold me responsible for your happiness. I'm not going to be *made* responsible. I want to live my own life. I am not going to alter myself in the slightest degree for you.

Dan has deliberately chosen to present Alan Matsen as coming from a background identical to his own. He is an ex-schoolteacher, a communist, a working class boy made good, a man who has had no experience with women, and is frightened by them. What we have here is Dan analysing himself in terms of his past life and experiences and trying to resolve his own psychological problems. He delves into his childhood, looks at his relationship with his family, considers why he lacks confidence and self-worth. In the confines of the prison camp, a totally artificial world, he has the opportunity to indulge in self-analysis and the roots of his love for David. Alan's private thoughts are expressed at length. He spends many hours wallowing in misery, as in this example.

What is the use? The little things - how when I sat on his bed he got up and crossed to the window and stayed there talking to John Flem. No for me, yes for everybody else. Always. What can I do but go away and hide myself in a corner. And then the thought of him back in the room, laughing and talking with the others. Oh Jesus, what will become of me? If the armistice came tomorrow I should be terrified to go away from him.

Better be as peaceful as possible. I shall lie on my back with a tranquil expression and close my eyes to prevent people coming and talking: and think of endless conversations wherein, sooner or later, he says the things I want him to say, he gives me rest at last, he takes my hand, puts his arms round my shoulders, and says, "Poor devil, give up struggling, I'll love you".

However, we must remember the book is a combined effort and David Dowie also is involved in the telling of Alan's story. His diary entries, in which he recounts the frustrations and anxieties caused by Alan's persistent attentions, provide a balance to such emotional wallowings.

Alan is barren. He has a life of his own. A parasite that sucks life from me. He couldn't understand the satisfaction I get from playing Rugger on a half-sized, sunbaked pitch as hard as a rock under a midsummer Italian sun. Mad? Yes. But a release - an escape from prison. An escape from Alan.

This section of the book is not as one-sided or intense as this account might make it seem. Although Alan's problems dominate, the other characters all play their own parts, and there is humour and action too: escape attempts, various camp rackets and activities, the outside world as seen from the orphanage windows, and more importantly news of the progress of the war. The prisoners were well supplied with accurate information and were fully aware of Italy's precarious position in the Axis.

As the summer progressed, it became clear that Italy was on its way out of the war and it seemed that release could be imminent. A surge of hope passed through Camp 49 and everybody's spirits were lifted. For Dan and David this meant a rush to finish *The Cage*. They laid great importance on it being a living account, written while they were experiencing the life they described, so it was vital to conclude the story before they went home. They managed it, fortunately, but the final chapters are obviously rushed and the sketches disappear from the manuscript. The Alan - David relationship had to be resolved and it is, but in rather a contrived way. Alan drops his role of hang-dog misery, and accepts that David has a fiancée whom he plans to marry; David's aversion to Alan's demands falls away and the two accept a closeness and friendship that they can both feel comfortable with. It is not wholly satisfactory; one cannot help but feel that Alan would never accept less than full commitment from David to the exclusion of everything else, but nevertheless the story is rounded off neatly with the words, "For us the war was over". And it looked as though it was. Dan and David could now prepare for the end of their imprisonment and the next stage in their lives.

★★★

The first hint that things were happening in Italy had come early in July, when one of the men burst in, "Boys, we've landed in Sicily. Just heard it on the news." (Almost every prison camp in Italy had its hidden radio). What excitement. The prisoners drew maps and eagerly marked on them the British advance across the island. A fortnight later, with the news of the fall of Palermo and three-quarters of Sicily shaded in on their maps, they were exultant. But Dan wrote in his notebook, "We draw no conclusions. Fourteen months of prison have taught us elementary patience."

Then on 25th July came the news of the resignation of Mussolini and the formal dissolution of the Fascist Party. Dan wrote, "We can't help being obscurely thrilled. We seem actually to have seen in the last week, the great coloured snake History wriggling past us. We have seen the year twist and turn and take a new direction." That morning Dan had been one of a group taken out for a walk in the neighbourhood,

.... the villagers looked at us with a queer, humorous curiosity. Everyone, they and us, felt a bubbling, champagne-sense of excitement. John could not stop giggling ... and some of the village girls were infected by it and giggled as well. On the other hand, the grass and the trees went on growing as usual, the sky was cloudy but not portentous, and a bird in the hedge sang very much as if nothing very important had happened.

Dan was as anxious as any of the prisoners to go home to his family but he realised that readjustment after the war was not going to be easy. For him prison-camp life had been fulfilling and productive. He had written two exceptional books; and he had fallen in love, resolving the difficulties which this created so that he was now enjoying the most important relationship of his life. Furthermore, he had been looked up to and respected by his fellow prisoners. He was considered an authority on many subjects and was often asked to help prisoners with essays and stories they were writing. His literature classes, his entertaining monologues, his sense of humour, and his role as friend and counsellor to those who needed advice all contributed to the high regard in which he was held. Undoubtedly he had been far more successful as a prisoner-of-war than ever he had been as an officer on the battlefield.

He was confident that his future lay in writing, but he realised it was not going to be easy to take up the strings of a literary career which had only just started. He had no idea in which direction he was going - so far he had been dabbling in a great many ponds - and he was fully aware that he was a long way from making a living as a writer. He was very ambitious - not for fame or public acclaim - but to write what he felt was the truth, the very essence of himself. He had been struggling with this problem during the writing of *The Cage*. One notebook entry reads,

> How shall I get the essential, nagging soul of me, the truth itself, out? ... I don't know what's inside me. The chaos when I look into my own personality. The conflict! Yet somewhere there behind the fog of spiritual war is the thing itself, the heart and true motive of my life, crying for my attention, imploring me to find it, recognise it, and express it. Damn the public, damn the publisher, this book will only have done its job for me if I can find myself in it, and write down in ink the essential that I live for.

His pre-war teaching days seemed very far away and the fervour with which he had promulgated his unorthodox methods was somewhat dimmed after his intervening experiences. Nevertheless he realised he would have to go back to teaching to earn enough money to live on.

Balanced against the problems of his career were those of his personal life. He was approaching the age of 30, but he still felt immature, indecisive and very much dependent on his family. Was he going to join them in Yeovil, in a house and a town that were utterly strange to him? He loved his parents and sisters and cared for them very much but he realised how inhibiting his dependence on them could be. In one sense he was the anchor, the strong one who looked after them, but in another he was the child who needed to be drawn in to the warmth of their close circle, comforted, loved and cherished. As far as he had any plans at all, judging by the comments in his letters home, he was going to apply for a teaching job in Yeovil and take it from there.

By comparison, his fellow prisoners all seemed to have ready-made lives to go back to. Many had wives and most had careers waiting for them. David was going to marry Jill and resume his job in town planning in Essex. George Mathieson was returning to his wife, Mary. He actually wrote a piece, at Dan's request which is included in *The Cage*, describing his proposal of marriage to her; they were at a summer music school, sipping cocoa on the balcony as they looked down on the chamber orchestra's rehearsal. Now he was going home to Mary and a three year old son, also George, whom he had never seen. And his job in the family firm was waiting for him.

In spite of his feelings for David, and a clear awareness of his own homosexuality, Dan accepted that he would have to marry when he returned to England, although he regarded it as a duty, and one to which he was not looking forward. Finding the right girl and coming to terms with married life was not going to be easy. But Dan was nothing if not brave. He was a man who saw the next step ahead, and however distasteful or difficult it might seem, if he felt that was the right thing to do, he did it. Going to war was a good example, and marrying was for him just another hurdle to be surmounted. He wrote in his notebook during the last weeks of his imprisonment,

I'll have to get married. Because what's the good of kidding myself I want to go back. Shops and trams and English voices and money in my pocket. But it needs more than that to make a life. ... Never left the family circle. Still a child at twenty-nine. ... But unless you go out from the family and love someone else - as they had to do - you'll never even understand them, never mind love them. ... Male spinster. Not that. Not that. ... The courage to give yourself to somebody else is the primary requisite. And no nonsense postponing the business till you find the One who can be trusted. That's more procrastination and cowardice. Risk refusal. If it did happen, it's better to have the gift of yourself returned than never to offer.

So it was with a sense of unease, as well as anticipation, that Dan prepared for his release from prisoner-of-war Camp 49 at Fontanellato.

Chapter 19

On the run

During that baking hot summer, heat wave conditions even by Italian standards, news filtered into the camp from the outside world. The *Corriere della Sera* was regularly available and it was from this newspaper that they learned on 25th July, of the fall of Mussolini, and the instigation of Marshal Badoglio as leader of the government in his place. It was obvious to all that his task was to take Italy out of the war, but signing an armistice is a complicated business, which could take a month or more to finalise. Dan was as excited as anybody at the turn events had taken, but he was particularly exultant at the fall of Fascism. This is what he wrote in his notebook. (The other old man is Victor Emmanuel).

> Coo, but you should have seen the newspapers! Three-inch headlines, and pictures of two old men who are, it seems, going to look after forty million Italians. They'll have their old hands full. Neither of them looks particularly competent to look after himself. Not a word from Mussolini apart from the fact that he's resigned. So after his twenty-one year strong man act, Mussolini takes the world's quickest curtain. After assuring mankind for twenty-one years that it was eternal, Fascism has vanished in a day.

However for the prisoners, life went on much as before, except the pictures of Mussolini disappeared and the guards became more friendly and ceased their practice of firing at any man who leaned out of the window. News came that the German and Italian forces in North Africa had surrendered and the war in the desert was over. On 10th July the Allies had landed in Sicily and were sweeping it clear of all enemy troops. The next step would be to invade the mainland of Italy and advance north to push back the Germans. Nobody in Camp 49 doubted that release was imminent; speculation was rife and spirits were high.

The senior officers met to decide their strategy. Instructions from the War Office had been circulated to all camps that in the case of an Italian armistice, all prisoners were to remain where they were and wait for the arrival of the Allied forces. In many camps this is what happened, but the men at Fontanellato were fortunate in having a far-sighted Senior British Officer, Lt.-Col. Hugo de Burgh. He realised how uncertain the situation was and decided to make sure they were ready to meet any eventuality. Roll-call, formerly a shambles of an affair conducted by the Italians with little co-operation from the prisoners, was now organised by the British officers. The men assembled in five companies, each with their own Commander and Adjutant. They were ordered to tidy up their appearance, for example beards were forbidden, and to have a decent set of clothes in reserve. Discipline was tightened and morale was high. Emergency supplies for a possible period on the run were hoarded, friends made plans to travel together and there was a voluntary increase in PT and Italian lessons.

The hot weather continued through August and into September. News came that the Allied forces had landed in the toe of Italy, but that was over a thousand miles away. In the vicinity of Fontanellato, there was an increase in heavily armed German patrols, who did not look as though they were about to withdraw. Then on the evening of 8th September 1943, came the sensational news of the Armistice. The local villagers were celebrating the festival of *Santa Maria Immaculata* on the green beside the convent. Noise and shouting from there was the first indication that something had happened, and then prison camp guards who had been attending the festival came rushing back waving their arms and yelling "Armistizio, Armistizio!" Inside the camp, games of bridge and rehearsals for the play, *Czarina*, were abandoned. Lt.-Col. de Burgh, after conferring with the Italian officers, spoke to the whole body of men assembled in the main hall and confirmed that the Armistice had indeed been signed. When the cheering had died down, he told them that the Germans were pouring troops into northern Italy, but that their Italian Commandant was not planning to hand the camp over to them. All were instructed to pack, ready for an early departure, and to get a good night's sleep. Wine was declared off ration in the bar and most men spent the evening celebrating and estimating how long it would be before they were home; two weeks did not seem an impossibility.

9th September dawned fine with the promise of another hot day. The SBO assembled all officers and men at 0900 hours. He told them that Germans were massing in the area, with the probable intention of transporting all prisoners of war back to Germany. The Commandant, Colonello Vicedomini, had sent out scouts to ascertain the enemy's position and should they be seen approaching, the bugle would sound the order to leave the camp. They were to march out in companies in an orderly manner and would assemble at a location some distance away which had been reconnoitred for them by the second-in-command, Capitano Camino. All were to wear battledress, to carry a small pack of essential equipment and to be ready to move at any moment. The men were told that once outside the camp they would remain together until they were given orders to disperse.

Lt.-Col. de Burgh was disregarding the War Office instructions by these orders, but it was fortunate for those prisoners at Fontanellato that he took this initiative and that he had the backing and support of the Italian officers in this. Many other prison camps remained closed and were taken over immediately by the Germans.

The first sign of activity was when a group of Italian guards came out into the compound at the back of the orphanage and cut a wide gap in the fence at the bottom of the playing field. The prisoners spent the morning in preparations and around midday, just as they were queueing up to go into the mess for lunch, the bugles sounded three Gs, signalling extreme urgency, and the evacuation began. They were about to leave the building when a German aircraft, a Junkers 52 troop carrier, screamed in very low over the camp, but it passed, and the men lined up in companies on the playing field ready to march out. Ronnie Noble, former war correspondent, had his camera returned to him by the Commandant so that he was able to photograph the exodus from the other side of the fence. And a very orderly, smart, *British* job they made of it. Michael Gilbert, after three weeks in the sick bay suffering from a massive carbuncle in his armpit, was on his feet, although not at all well. The other invalid, Eric Newby, who had broken his ankle on the treacherous marble staircase ten days before, rode out on a mule, led by an Italian guard. In the baking midday sun, they followed Camino to the hiding place the Italians had found for them. This was about three miles away among vineyards and fields of tall maize in an area concealed by a high embankment and a row of poplars. They quickly spread out over an area of about half a mile square and hid among the shade of bushes and vines, with the SBO's headquarters established in a dry river bed in the middle. All had gone according to plan and it seemed they had got out undetected. They had been observed by a few local peasants on the way, who seemed friendly, although tense, and had greeted them with words of encouragement. The only worrying incident was the appearance of another German plane which had passed over very low causing everyone to dive for cover, but it departed as quickly as it had come.

For the rest of the day they lay concealed, over six hundred men, lying as still as possible, waiting for nightfall. Someone produced a copy of the *Corriere della Sera* with its four inch high headline ARMISTIZIO. But it did not give them any real news beyond the fact that Marshal Badoglio had surrendered unconditionally and for Italy the war was over. Still, spirits were high among the prisoners, who had no doubt that the British troops would soon arrive to drive the Germans out. Sea landings at Genoa and Rimini seemed a certainty, backed up by airborne landings at Milan and Rome. In fact, the British Eighth Army was a thousand miles away, fighting its way up through Calabria, and the only landing planned was that of the Fifth Army now on its way to Salerno in the far south. The German troops were pouring in to confront them and it would be another eighteen months before the whole of Italy was in the hands of the Allies.

But they did have more positive news about what was happening at the orphanage. Camino and Stuart Hood, who was an expert linguist, had been back to investigate. They discovered that a few minutes after they had left the camp, a large contingent of German troops had arrived, ransacked the building, taken the Commandant prisoner and left. The villagers were understandably nervous and were keeping well out of the way. But it was the Commandant, Colonello Vicedomini, who had to face the wrath of the Germans. He had done all he could to help the prisoners to escape and for that he was tortured and imprisoned and although he returned to the area at the end of the war, he was a broken, sick man who did not live long afterwards. Many ex-49ers have paid tribute to his courage.

The SBO gave orders that the unit was to remain where it was for the night. The outlying men moved in to the river bed, where a meal of bread, cheese and salami was handed out before they settled down to sleep. In the warm night air, explosions could be heard in the distance and there was the constant hum of heavy traffic moving along the Via Emilia, the main road which runs through the Po valley from Rimini to Milan. Nearer at hand was the occasional roar of a motor cycle; there was no doubt that the Germans were on the move.

On 10th September, they awoke to a misty start and the uncertainty of what was to happen next. Return to the orphanage was clearly impossible with so many Germans in the area. Thanks to the support of the villagers, no hint of their whereabouts had been given to the enemy. And the locals were to be of more practical help as well, for during the morning a constant stream of farmers and peasants arrived at their hiding place bringing food and provisions of all kinds. They had been responsible for last night's supper; now they cycled out, bringing not only the local produce, but tins of condensed milk, sugar, butter, bully-beef, all salvaged from the prison camp. They had gone in to collect what they could find as soon as the Germans had left. Cigarettes and tobacco from the same source were also handed over. In fact there was so much that an official distribution point had to be arranged. It was difficult to remember that forty-eight hours earlier, these people were the enemy. Now they couldn't be more kind and friendly, risking their necks to hand over provisions which they badly needed themselves. Further help was provided in the shape of civilian clothing, of all descriptions, mainly the worse for wear and mostly in small sizes, but it meant that anyone who wanted to could collect a pair of trousers, jacket and hat to disguise himself.

In their desire to be helpful, the local Italians also brought good news of the Allies' progress, such optimistic reports of landings all along both coasts and the rapid advance of the British army from the south that it seemed as though help were close at hand. But it was all false, as they discovered when an officer was sent off to listen to the BBC news in a neighbouring farmhouse.

Towards evening, the SBO announced that any officer who wished to leave could do so. They were advised to form themselves into groups of four, and to carry some form of identification. Most were already dressed in civilian clothes, but wisely they kept their own boots and underclothes. It was a ragged, furtive-looking lot of scarecrows that were led off in small groups by Camino and other Italian helpers to be placed in temporary accommodation for the night. As the light faded they bedded down in haylofts, outhouses, and cellars ready for the next stage in the adventure.

Next morning the hundreds of former prisoners had spread out and melted into the countryside. This was the fertile plain of the Po Valley, an area dotted with small farms, linked by winding country roads. The flat land was criss-crossed with drainage ditches and streams flowing between vineyards and fields of maize. The local peasants, mainly women and old men, cultivated the land in the way it had been done for centuries, back breaking physical work for very small rewards. These were the people who, as a body, rose to help the escapees in spite of terrible warnings issued by the Germans. Why were the Italian peasants so hospitable and supportive? It has been suggested that it was because their real enemy was, and had been for centuries, Authority. Traditionally this came in the shape of the landlord and the system of land tenure which held them in its grip of poverty. The Pope was a figure equally to be feared and the authority of the Catholic Church all powerful. Then, with the war Mussolini took over the role, and once he fell, the Germans and the Fascists became the enemy. So the peasants rallied in their support of the prisoners on the run. And in spite of the fact that it was very dangerous, it was also exciting to be involved in the action, to be part of a shared conspiracy, entertaining these strange, fresh-faced men with their broken Italian, in the grip of a euphoria brought on by their sudden freedom. In addition, many of them had members of their own family on the run, deserters from the Italian army or young men fleeing the Germans intent on transporting them to labour camps. So they did their best to help the Allied escapers in the hope that somebody somewhere was helping their boys.

Dan and David of course stayed together. They were looked after initially by the Meletti family who had a small farm on the outskirts of Soragna, a village about five miles north-west of Fontanellato. The Melettis were kindness itself and protected the boys from the Germans and Italian fascists who were combing the area for escapees. The two slept in the hayloft but spent the daytime hiding, sometimes in thick woodland or even in a ditch, where they were urgently finishing off the last chapter of *The Cage*. They were in contact with friends from the camp who were staying with other families nearby. During the first weeks they regularly spent their days with John Mills and another officer and shared the midday meal brought out to them by their hosts. But John and his friend became restless and decided to strike out south and make their way towards the Allied lines. They left Dan and David in good spirits planning to follow them shortly. Their first priority was to finish their book.

Dan's Italian was not as good as he thought, but it rapidly improved as he and David made friends with the Meletti family and their neighbours. They were all interested in what they were writing and looked with awe at the loose-leaf sheets now sewn into a book, which contained many illustrations of the camp and the countryside. Dan handed over this and the nine exercise books containing the manuscript of *The Trap* to Dino Meletti, who took the responsibility very seriously, promising to keep them safe and post them to Dan in England once the war was over.

There were still many English ex-prisoners hiding in the area; Dan and David frequently met up with John Fleming and Alec Harding who were staying a few miles up the road at Roncole di Busseto. They often spent evenings there, at the farm of Benvenuto Fontanella, drinking red wine and socialising with the villagers, Dan's charm and amusing conversation by now coming over very well in Italian. It seems he made good friends wherever he went, and once again, he swapped addresses and promised to write.

But it was time to move on. *The Cage* was finished and Dan felt happy that both his manuscripts were in safe hands. News of the Allied advance was not good and they knew that if they were going to reach the British forces, currently stuck just north of Naples, they had better get started on their long walk before the winter weather closed in. So in early October 1943, Dan and David, together with John Fleming and Alec Harding, said farewell to their Italian friends and headed for the Apennines. There were hugs and kisses and promises to keep in touch and the tears coursed down Signora Meletti's face as she said goodbye to Dan, her special favourite.

★★★

After the war, many of those ex-prisoners who were at large in Italy related their adventures and all tell a similar story. All pay tribute to the kindness and generosity of the Italians who sheltered and fed them, at great danger to themselves. Anyone found harbouring an ex-POW was likely to be shot by the Germans. But most went out of their way to help, hiding them in haylofts, offering them food and clothes and giving them directions to another sympathetic family. These people were terribly poor and had barely enough for themselves; many of them were also hiding Italian deserters, often members of their own family, who were on the run from the Germans.

The decision the escapees had to make was whether to head for the British lines, as Dan did, or to stay put and wait for help to arrive. Those who chose the former option faced an arduous journey south, of over a thousand miles, and they had to keep to the remoter ridges of the Apennine mountains to avoid the Germans who were out in force rounding up Allied prisoners, Americans, Canadians, South Africans, as well as British. Some attempted to travel north across The Alps into neutral Switzerland, or west to the Mediterranean coast trusting in the rumour that Allied landings were expected there. A number of Fontanellato prisoners were successful in getting to Swizerland, including Lt.-Col. Hugo de Burgh who had the most hazardous crossing of the Grenz Glacier, where he stumbled into a deep crevass and was rescued by locals just in time before becoming frozen into the solid ice.

It was estimated that in the autumn of 1943 there were over eleven thousand ex-prisoners in Italy from camps all over the country. Many slipped comfortably into the Italian way of life. Some settled down with Italian families to see the

south when they stopped for the night. They were offered hospitality by peasants, priests, monks, even charcoal burners; they bumped into a group of partisans, deserters from the Alpini regiment, but declined to join them. They were briefly captured by a lone German, whom they murdered. And all the time it rained, generally non-stop. There were times when they longed to stay put; Michael Gilbert was specially tempted by a monastery on Monte Catria, which they approached as night fell, guided by organ music. But they pushed on towards the Allied lines, heartened by the sight of Spitfires overhead and easier flatter terrain as they neared the south. By the end of October they reached the Sangro River where they camped on the hillside, looking down on the British lines. Germans were everywhere. Next morning, together with a South African ex-prisoner called Hal Becker, they crossed the river and rushed the lines. Michael and Toby got through to safety, but Hal was killed. Tony was shot in the foot and captured and spent the rest of the war a prisoner in Germany.

Captain Philip Gardner was another of the POWs who emerged from the camp at Fontanellato. With two pals, Percy Gers and a Canadian, Jimmy Gardner (no relation), he lived for a while with local farmers waiting for the Allies to arrive. At the end of September, they became impatient and decided to head south to meet them. Their experiences were very similar to those already described. Crossing roads, busy with German troops, was a major problem; often they crawled through the culverts underneath. They were still in uniform, albeit disguised by having been dyed black, but the colour tended to run in the rain. Generally they were well received by the Italians and did their bit to pay for their board by helping out where they could. Treading the grapes and dancing later at the harvest party with purple-stained bare feet was just one example. They really struck lucky one Sunday evening when, recognised for what they were by their attire, they were invited to rest in a cowshed. After an anxious wait, a smartly dressed maid appeared carrying a folded card-table, which she set up and proceeded to lay with a starched white table-cloth, fine glasses and silver cutlery. Then, to their amazement, she served them a sumptuous meal and several bottles of vintage wine. Next morning they met the master of the property, a rich cycle manufacturer, who kitted them out with smart civilian clothing and gave them three new bicycles. After this they felt so confident that they cycled right through the centre of Florence instead of skulking round the edge as they had planned. Eventually, as they worked their way higher into the Apennines, the bikes proved impractical and they swapped them for mountain boots. But this had given them a really good start, and before long they were within sight of Rome, where they were lucky enough to encounter Major Sam Derry who had known Pip Gardner in Chieti prison camp. Major Derry was the leader of a huge escape organisation for Allied prisoners of war; this was based in Rome and used the Vatican as a refuge. They had 3925 successful escapes on their books by the end of hostilities. Pip was found digs in Rome with others in the same position, and in the meantime, while waiting for escape instructions, they lived in comparative luxury. On 1st January 1944, two of them went to the Opera House, wearing newly acquired Italian suits and accompanied by a couple of Yugoslav girls. They sat in the sixth row of the stalls to hear *La Traviata* with Benjamino Gigli and his daughter Rina. (How Dan would have enjoyed that evening!) The theatre was swarming with high-ranking Germans and Italians and they were surprised to meet some other British officers there too, also disguised. But Pip Gardner's luck was not to last. On 8th January he was arrested and sent to the notorious "Regina Coeli" jail, facetiously nicknamed the Queen of Heaven because it was so awful, before being transported via Germany to Czechoslovakia, where he spent the rest of the war in a prison camp.

Those who were at liberty long enough had the rigours of winter weather to contend with. In the mountains the snow came early and the cold was relentless. Private Vic Wilson and his pal Reg spent nine months on the run before crossing the British lines to safety. They suffered terribly from cold, illness and hunger, and were reduced at one low point to eating meat torn from a dead sheep. (A similar dead sheep occurs in a number of accounts and seems to have achieved almost mythical status.) It was a cold New Year for them as they spent the whole of 1st January 1944 buried in the snow on the hillside above the village where they had been staying, hiding from the Germans who were searching the area. They too were full of praise for the generosity of the Italian people who sheltered and encouraged them. At one farm they met a lady, originally from Oldham who gave them Brooke Bond tea; she had married an Italian ice-cream seller and returned with him to Italy.

Lieutenant Ian Bell was another prisoner from Camp 49 who later wrote about his experiences on the run. In fact he was arrested early on and taken to a transit camp at Parma, where there were prisoners of many nationalities, including large numbers of Italian deserters who were particularly badly treated, and American air crew who had baled out. Conditions were appalling; they were guarded by fierce black alsatian dogs, and so it was with some relief that they learned that they were to be transported to Mantua. In the confusion at the station, Bell seized the opportunity to escape, by climbing onto the axle of a moving goods train. This took him south over the River Po and as it slowed, he dropped off into the countryside near Bologna. After a brief meal of raw potatoes and withered grapes, he was on his way. He struggled up into the foothills of the Apennines into a sparsely populated area where weeks later, barefoot and starving, he found himself surrounded by a group of the toughest, most evil looking men imaginable. In complete silence, they each covered him with a rifle. It was with relief that he realised that these were neither Germans nor Fascists but partisans, who after extensive questioning accepted his story. They were men from the remains of the Alpini Regiment, determined to fight the Germans to the end. (Could this have been the same group that Tony Davies encountered?) As they had ample food supplies, Ian Bell decided to stay with them for a few days. In fact it was not long before he agreed to join them and to become their leader.

This must have been one of the better disciplined groups of partisans. They were well organised with a strict training programme, and Bell, keen to get back into the fight against the Germans, continued with them for some weeks, planning their campaigns together with the Sergeant-Major in a mixture of Italian and English. They were successful in raiding German goods trains, capturing weapons and ammunition, destroying bridges and other strategic points. More recruits, local people and army deserters, joined until the band, originally fifty-five men, had increased to about 450. Hidden in the mountain passes they were a force to be reckoned with. They engaged in battle with the Germans sent out to eliminate them, and with a wide-spread intelligence network and support from the local peasants they were very successful. They even succeeded in blowing up a troop train. This was when Bell decided to leave and continue his journey to the west coast where he hoped to find a boat to take him to Corsica, which by this time had fallen to the Allies. He got as far as the coastal town of Imperia, where he was arrested by the Italian police who had been alerted by Fascists. And so he ended up back in Mantua, and thence to a prison camp in Czechoslovakia.

★★★

Families back home waited anxiously for news, unaware what the situation in Italy was and very much afraid for the young men who had disappeared. The last letter Dan's parents received from the camp at Fontanellato was dated 15.8.43 and arrived in Yeovil a month later. After that there was not a word.

Chapter 20

No news

All the Billanys could do was wait. The Italian situation was very unclear and the advice to relatives was to keep sending mail to the last prisoner-of-war camp address, letters to be limited to one a fortnight. Of course there was nobody left at the orphanage in Fontanellato, and no chance that mail would be delivered to Dan, but Harry did not know that and he kept on writing. News of home, the garden, the books he had read and the films he had seen; news of Hatchitts and Uncle Joe; news of the family - Joan and her horse and her boyfriends, - Eva and Kit, and another baby expected soon, - Mother, still in poor health but better than last year. And most exciting news of all, the publication at last of *The Magic Door*, just in time for Christmas and "selling like hot cakes". All this information, written in Harry's neat copperplate, went off to be read and censored, stored somewhere or other, and returned years later by the Red Cross or the Allied Forces when they finally gained control of Italy.

But on the more positive side, Harry was able to correspond with the families of other prisoners. George Mathieson's wife and David Dowie's mother were already in his address book as they had been in the habit of exchanging news received in letters from Italy. Before long, a network had been set up between the families of Camp 49ers, consoling and encouraging each other and passing on every piece of good news.

It was Harry who took responsibility for letter writing, but on 14th November 1943, Dan's thirtieth birthday, each member of the family wrote a paragraph. They all wished him "Many Happier Returns of the Day" and this comment from Eva summed up the general feeling, "We are all longing to hear that you are safe and well, and keep on hoping that you will be with us soon. Keep smiling old man, it won't be long now." But the letter was never delivered.

On 13th December, a postcard arrived from Mary Mathieson to say she had received information from the War Office that her husband George was on his way home. He had reached the south of Italy and rejoined the British troops. He arrived in England on 5th January and immediately wrote to the Billanys to enquire about Dan and to reassure them that he was fit and well when they had parted. He spoke warmly of their friendship, saying what a fine chap Dan was, looked up to and respected by all.

Dan was always in the nature of a public figure: in the camp it was impossible to know everyone but I feel sure everyone knew Dan. I don't mean that he courted publicity, but that for example he was looked up to as an authority on almost any subject. I haven't heard the BBC Brains Trust, so I won't say he was the camp Joad (I don't think that's fair to either Dan or Joad) but perhaps there is a parallel ...

George Mathieson and his companion, Joe Drayson (G B Drayson who later became MP for Harrogate), had made the long journey through Italy in awful conditions, wading through swollen rivers, hiding in culverts, resting up with Italian families before making their way along the high Apennine ridge. But they had been lucky and reached the British lines in record time. Now they were allowed twenty-eight days leave and double the normal rations before rejoining the Royal Artillery.

Gradually news filtered through of others, some now prisoners of the Germans, but at least alive and able to write home. Some had made it to the British lines, but there was no news of Dan and David. They had not been seen since 10th September. Still Harry went on writing; it had become a point of honour with him not to give up, to keep Dan alive by talking to him once a fortnight in this way. Right through that winter and the following summer, his letters, each one numbered as Dan had asked, continued. He passed on family news: the birth of Eva's second son, Peter Julian in November '43; Joan's marriage in June '44, not to Ken, but to Gerald Brake, a Somerset farmer; regular bulletins about Mother's health; and his own ongoing battle for a disability pension. And there was news too of all Dan's friends, who were urgently enquiring about him, of the sales of his books and hopes for the future. Harry concludes his letter of Jan. 3rd 1944, "My God, and won't there be a yell of joy when we get a line from you. Cheer up Son. Love Mother, Joan, Bonzo and Dad." He always included Bonzo in the signing off. But as time went by with no news, despair started to break into the pseudo-cheerful tone.

Early in 1944, Harry began pestering the War Office, the Red Cross, the Foreign Office, anyone who he could think of, for news of his son. They were polite and acknowledged all his letters but could give no information about Dan or David Dowie. News came through of fellow prisoners. George Mathieson was assiduous in following up every lead and passing the information on. John Fleming was a prisoner in Oflag 9, John Mills and Donald Futrell in Oflag 79. Alec Harding was mistakenly reported to have been seen in a German prison camp, but then his wife had to suffer the disappointment of being told that this was not true, it must have been someone else. Jimmy Candler had walked into the British lines on 21st July after ten months on the run; G H Nicholls made it in four months and Gervase Craddock also, but it took him thirteen months. To Harry it did not seem impossible that Dan would turn up one day, so he continued to write, although less positively. "This is No. 80 and seems to be another one for the land of nowhere".

The Allies eventually drove the Germans out of Italy and in May 1945 the war in Europe ended, but there was still no word of Dan. On 19th June 1945, Harry placed an advertisement in the Daily Telegraph asking for news of Dan, and replies came pouring in but they were inconclusive. He had been seen in various places with David Dowie, in hiding, on his way south, he had his manuscript with him. All were encouraging and hopeful but no-one could give any recent information.

Finally Harry stopped writing and the whole family sank into despair. Even George's optimism was fading. This is a paragraph from his letter to Harry of 18th July 1946.

You have asked me for 'my own thoughts'. I hope what follows will not cause any pain, but on two or three occasions when we were in the mountains, Italians told us how the bodies of two English soldiers had been found up some mountain. They had died of exposure and were clasped together evidently in an attempt to keep warm. That always suggested Dan and David to me. The story was the sort that one never tracks down - first heard about Oct. 43 - supposed to be other ranks - but I mention this more as indicating the impression Dan and David's friendship had given me.

Chapter 21

When sorrows come...

"Oh Danny Boy, the pipes, the pipes are calling,
From glen to glen and down the mountainside.
The summer's gone, and all the flowers are dying
'Tis you must go and I must bide.

"But come ye back, when summer's in the meadow,
Or when the valley's hushed and white with snow,
'Tis I'll be here, in sunshine or in shadow -
Oh Danny Boy, Oh Danny Boy, I love you so ..."

Harry rose from the breakfast table, stumped across the room and switched off the wireless with a jerky movement. "Stupid song, stupid song," he muttered, as he sat down again. All three carried on with the meal, avoiding each other's eyes, the silence heavy around them.

★★★

In January 1946, Elsie Billany slipped on the hall floor made wet by trodden snow, fell heavily onto the tiles and broke her left hip. It was a tricky fracture and she was sent to Exeter hospital to have an operation pinning the bone. Poor Elsie, she seemed to have spent so much of her life in hospital and each time there were problems and painful complications. When she came back home, the local hospital in Yeovil took over her care. There must have been some wires crossed because the treatment they gave her was totally inappropriate, involving traction and physiotherapy which not only dislodged the pin, but dislocated her hip. The result was that she had to spend the next nine months in hospital, most of this time flat on her back with her left leg encased in plaster from hip to toe.

Eva's husband, Charles Wilkin was also in very poor health. He had been in and out of hospital for the past three years. Various treatments and minor operations had produced slight improvements but failed to sort out the trouble. Then early in 1946 he went into Hull Royal Infirmary for a gall-bladder operation. For a few days all seemed to go well and then with no warning, he died. It seemed that he had a spleen abnormality which had never been diagnosed and which had flared up under the rigours of the operation and killed him. Suddenly

Eva was left a widow with two small children. She took the obvious step and moved in with her family in Yeovil.

Fortunately Newlands was a big house. Joan and her husband Gerald were also living there as well as Harry, Elsie and of course Bonzo. And over them all hung an unspoken anxiousness, a sickening sense of loss always at the back of the mind, because there was still no news of Dan. Harry worked diligently making enquiries, writing letters, filing copies. It became a full time job bordering on obsession. But his searches continued to be fruitless. There was a moment of hope during the summer of 1945 when the War Office came up with some information that appeared to be reliable. Records showed that Lieutenants Dowie and Billany had been admitted to Mantua Hospital with slight injuries in December 1943. From there, they should have been transported to Germany, but as there was no record of them ever having arrived, the conclusion was that they had escaped in transit. This did not help the Billany family at all; it just widened the area of uncertainty. Years later the War Office admitted that a mistake had been made, they never were at Mantua.

Harry also handled business matters with the publishers and in an effort to further Dan's literary career, offered them some of his old manuscripts, together with discovered fragments of poems and political and literary essays from his university days. But they were not interested; it was too much of a rag-bag collection without focus. Dan had also mentioned in letters sent from the troopship that he had left some short stories with a literary agent in London. Harry contacted as many as he could but none had heard of Dan Billany. Everywhere he turned he seemed to draw a blank.

And then in November 1945, there arrived at Newlands a letter that raised everybody's spirits.

Dear Mr Dan.

Not having heard from you since the day you left, and being anxious for news of you, now that our poor country has been restored to some sort of freedom, we beg you to let us know how you are.

Hoping to have good news of you very soon, we send you our best wishes and kindest regards, and assure you that we shall always remember you.

Family Benevenuto Fontanella
Roncole di Busseto
Parma, Italy.

Of course the letter was in Italian and there was an anxious time while they were waiting for a translation. Harry immediately wrote back and it was established that Dan and David had stayed with this family, but they had had no news of them after they had left the area in October 1943.

In February 1946 another Italian letter arrived from a different source. Here

157

is the translation.

To the Family of Mr Dan Billany.

I the undersigned, wish to inform you that your son, Dan Billany a prisoner of war at the camp at Fontanellato was set free on the 8th Sept. 1943, the day of the Armistice.

He arrived at my house with a friend, a certain David who stayed nearly a month. Afterwards as the Germans were combing the area, he had to leave my house and take refuge elsewhere.

Since then we have heard nothing about them. I am in possession of some books belonging to him and, as I had arranged to send them on, when the war was over, I sent a letter some months ago but got no reply. I hope this one will reach you safely and that your son will be there to reply to me himself.

With kindest regards from,

Dino Meletti
No. 211 Via Farnese
Soragna
Parma, Italy.

News of the manuscripts was good news indeed. Dan had written warmly about both books in his letters home and the family knew how important they were. During the next couple of months Harry and his translator had a busy correspondence with both families, and other Italian friends that Dan had made in the area, recalling happy evenings in sadder times. The culmination was the receipt of a parcel from Dino Meletti containing thirteen handwritten books, the manuscripts of *The Trap* and *The Cage*. They arrived safely at Newlands on 21st March 1946.

There was still no news of Dan but these two manuscripts told the story of his whole life. *The Trap* must have made strange, painful reading for Harry, Elsie, Eva and Joan, for there they were, portrayed as the Pascoes; all the tiny details were accurate, only in the broad sweep had Dan fictionalised them. The only one whose name had not been changed was Bonzo who bounced throughout the story. The early days, the new home, the bombing and the injuries were all included. In the second part of the book, they read about Dan's life in the army - the sea journey, the war in the desert, the Battle of Gazala and capture. Much of this was familiar to the family through letters, although none had been received after his arrival at the front line. Now they could read what it had really been like and share the awful, painful experiences in Dan's compelling prose.

The Cage too made for strange reading. A weird feeling of *deja vu* hung over the family as they read the manuscript and examined the sketches. It echoed the letters they had received from the three POW camps, but here was the reality, much starker, everything seen in a stronger, harsher light. For all it was presented as fiction, this was the true picture of the eighteen months Dan and his friends had spent as prisoners of the Italians. The text is dominated by Dan's personality, almost as if he were there talking to them. They read separately and scarcely discussed what they were reading, each privately moved by a sudden closeness to Dan. There seemed now little hope that he would ever come back, but each member of the family kept such thoughts private and cherished the only link they had with their son and brother through his writing.

For Harry, the receipt of the texts gave a great boost to his flagging spirits. Immediately he set to, with earnest concentration, to type out the manuscripts in triplicate. And for months all his energies were directed at getting Dan's work into print.

He started with *The Cage*, the shorter of the two. David Dowie was co-author of this book and the text was written partly in his regular, light handwriting. The Billanys were well acquainted with David through Dan's letters; this was the man he had chosen for Joan to marry and whom he had described in glowing detail on several occasions. David too was still missing and his widowed mother, herself homeless and living temporarily with her daughter, was just as worried about the fate of her son. She and Elsie exchanged many letters sharing their worries and she was happy to leave all the business arrangements concerning the book to Harry. He chose the dedication which was to H. E. Wilson and F. E. Harley, the two authors' mothers, designated by their maiden names.

George Mathieson was also involved right from the start. He was only too willing to read the text and surprised to discover himself uncompromisingly portrayed as Henry. He was able to identify most of the other characters in the story, almost all based on real people. At Harry's request, he made detailed notes on a page by page basis and wrote a preface for the book.

By the end of August 1946 the typescript was ready and Harry confidently sent it to Fabers, together with the illustrations and George's additional material. But within a fortnight it had been rejected on the grounds that it was unevenly written, and there were too many POW stories on the market at the time. As it turned out, Fabers were to regret this decision.

It was Longmans, Green and Co., who agreed to publish in the end but not without reservations, (they were particularly worried about the problem of libel), and they decided they would delay for two years when it was felt that the public would be ready for war books again.

The Cage was eventually published on 23rd May 1949. During the long period of preparation Harry was in almost weekly correspondence with Mark Longman, director of the publishers, who consulted him on every detail: cuts to the text, alterations, a preface, the dust jacket, and the question of whether to include Dan's sketches and his and David's photos. Harry was all for using Dino Meletti's letter, both in Italian and translation, by way of introduction, and he fought hard to retain the sketches and to include photographs. Mark Longman was the essence of politeness and good manners, enquiring regularly about Harry's own health which was not good at this time and about Mrs Billany's injured leg, still causing her trouble. But he had the final say. The sketches were not included but photographs of Dan and David were printed on the frontispiece with the comment "whose fates are unknown". On the following page was an autobiographical note about them and the circumstances under which the book had been written. For the dust jacket, they used a reproduction of the wrapping paper in which the parcel of books had been sent from Italy, and inside it was a plea for anyone who had information about the authors to communicate with the publishers. The book was an immediate success and attracted rave reviews all round the world and interest from America in the film rights. Harry proudly despatched copies to all Dan's friends and, with the help of Romeike & Curtice's press-cuttings agency, began collecting reviews. To take one example, H E Bates, writing in The Sunday Times, concludes with this paragraph.

Who were these young men? Why did we never hear of them before? They had remarkable gifts; their writing has astonishing maturity. It seems incredible that this document, so vivid and assured and without the faintest sign in it of the perfunctory amateur, can be, and must remain, their only published work. If they ever asked a memorial - and they would probably have blown a sustained raspberry in pidgin Italian at any such fatuous suggestion - they could hardly have asked for a better one than this. It is unique in that they not only made it themselves, but that, unlike those of commoner manufacture, it is completely worthy of them.

But Harry's euphoria was followed by deep depression. The strain and hard work of the last two and a half years had taken its toll on him and he became seriously ill with mental problems and a worsening of his heart condition. On 15th August 1946, the Billanys had been notified by the War Office that their son must now be officially presumed dead, but Harry never accepted it and kept expecting him to turn up; probably, he said, he was suffering from amnesia and had settled down with an Italian girl and was raising a family. But the truth was he had disappeared without trace and nobody seemed able to give a hint of what had happened to him.

Years earlier, Harry had typed up Dan's other manuscript, The Trap, ready to submit once The Cage was published. But by this time he was not well enough to undertake the negotiations and it was Joan who had to deal with the publishers. In June 1949 she sent the typescript to Longmans, but to everyone's surprise it was turned down. (Could it have been dealing with Harry that was the disincentive?) However, Fabers snapped it up immediately, having been very impressed with the success of The Cage. This time preparations went ahead quickly and by the end of the year Harry's health was improved and he was thoroughly involved again.

The note in *The Cage* asking for information about the authors was a good selling point. Almost all the reviewers mention it and of course it added poignancy to the story to know that the authors, who were also the two main characters, were still missing. Moreover it did bring a response. Within a week of publication, Mark Longman received a visit from a young man called T W Spencer, who worked in a nearby office, where he had that morning seen a copy of *The Cage* and recognised Dan and David's photographs. He had a strange story to tell. He too was an ex-POW who after the Italian Armistice wandered aimlessly round the countryside for some time. Eventually he became ill and was taken to hospital in Fermo, a small town near the Adriatic coast, about 600 miles south of Fontanellato. There were many ex-prisoners in hiding in that part of the country, and there existed a network of communication between them and the Partisans. A certain Sergeant-Major "X" had turned informer and was circulating in the area giving information to the Germans about the whereabouts of British escapees. Ultimately it was decided he would have to be removed from the scene, so two of them lay in wait for him in the neighbouring village of Macerata. From their photographs, Spencer identified these two as Dan Billany and David Dowie. In the scuffle that ensued, one of the men, Billany, was seriously wounded by a hand grenade thrown by "X" and taken to the Civil Hospital in Fermo. Shortly afterwards he died of his wounds and Spencer arranged for his burial in a local cemetery and placed in the grave a bottle containing his papers and details of his story.

When they heard this the Billanys were very excited, Joan started making plans to visit the grave and Mark Longman wrote to the War Office asking permission to open it up and examine the contents of the bottle. Not unnaturally the War Office wanted to interview Spencer, but he proved to be most elusive, frequently changing address and failing to turn up for appointments. Eventually, at the War Office's instigation, the local Carabinieri at Fermo conducted an extensive search in the area for Dan's grave but no trace of it was found, and the matter was dropped. It was beginning to look like another false trail. Moreover, it seemed unlikely to his family that Dan would have involved himself in such violent retribution on a fellow soldier, but this was the only version of events that they had, so it was decided to include Spencer's story in the autobiographical note at the beginning of *The Trap*.

1950 was a disastrous year for the Billanys. Elsie was still suffering from the effects of her accident and now walked painfully with a stick and a built up shoe. Joan was badly incapacitated following a riding accident and an injury to her spine, but worst of all was Harry's condition. His obsessive behaviour was now becoming uncontrolled and he seemed to be teetering on the edge of complete mental breakdown. The crunch came when he insisted on returning to Hull. None of the family was well enough or willing to go with him, but he persuaded a visiting nurse to accompany him on the train. He travelled in his pyjamas and dressing gown, and this was what he was wearing when he arrived at Paragon

Station, where he was met by his brother Mick who took him back to his house in River Grove. This was only a matter of a couple of hundred yards away from 15 Lakeside Grove, the site of the bombing nine years earlier. Mick's family tried to look after him but it was impossible and so on 28th April 1950 he was admitted to De La Pole Mental Hospital, angry, impatient and suffering from delusions.

It was at about the same time that Roger M Keyes contacted Mrs Billany to say how much he had enjoyed reading *The Cage* and would she allow him to make enquiries in Italy about Dan's disappearance. She agreed, as did Mrs Dowie, but they did not set their hopes very high. Roger Keyes, a member of the BBC Foreign News Service, was a talented, solitary man, who committed suicide two years later. He was fired by the mystery and decided to combine his summer holiday in Italy with investigations. Prior to leaving he talked to everyone who might be able to help, including Dan's fellow prisoners-of-war, George Mathieson and John Fleming. He also managed to track down the elusive T W Spencer, who by this time had modified his account somewhat, but it was this story that Keyes decided to follow up. On 30th June, he set off for Italy with detailed descriptions of Dan and David Dowie, specimens of their handwriting and a selection of photographs.

Roger Keyes spent the next two weeks making meticulous enquiries in the Fermo and Macerata regions. He interviewed doctors and examined the hospital records, which showed that Spencer had been there and Sergeant-Major "X", the informer in his tale was indeed active in the region at the time. There had been many ex-POWs in the area some of whom were brought into the hospital with wounds of varying degrees of severity. But there was no record of the names Billany or Dowie. He showed their photographs to many local people who had been in the partisan movement or who had sheltered British soldiers, but nobody recognised them. Nor could he get any help from the police, the Town Hall or other local organisations. He sadly had to admit that he had drawn a complete blank. The only thing he could feel certain about was that Dan had not met his end in the way described by Spencer; indeed it seemed most unlikely that Dan and David had ever been in that part of Italy. He concluded his report, "It seems probable that, if any clues to their fate still exist, they will be found much further north - somewhere between Modena and Bologna, where Billany and Dowie were last seen by John Fleming in October 1943." Another disappointment and the family were once again left with the empty feeling of uncertainty.

On the 10th June 1950, while Roger Keyes was making his enquiries, a War Memorial to the Teachers of Hull was unveiled in the Art College on Anlaby Road. Dan Billany's name was second on the plaque. The family was invited to attend the ceremony, but Harry was by now in the throes of a mental breakdown, still refusing to believe that Dan was dead, and none of the others was well enough or had the heart to journey to Hull.

In August *The Trap* was published as planned with Spencer's story included in *The Note on the Author* and the year of Dan's death given as 1945; Harry had insisted on changing this from 1944 before he went into hospital. The book was an immediate success, widely and favourably reviewed and it was not long before talk of film rights, translations and new editions followed. In fact the film rights never materialised, but it was translated into several languages, including Polish, and it was later issued as a Readers Union book.

Harry was very pleased to receive his copy in the hospital and started collecting reviews. His mind was constantly on his family, disturbed by worries about their health and anxious for news of his two grandsons. And especially his thoughts were with Dan. He kept with him the green press cuttings book, in which he had pasted all Dan's notices, beginning with letters he had written to The Hull Daily Mail as a boy, and including reviews of his books and articles about his disappearance. Sadly, he did not get round to pasting in the reviews of *The Trap*.

He longed to see Elsie and his daughters, but it was too far for them to travel. So it was a great relief to them all when, at the beginning of October, he was transferred to the Tone Vale Mental Hospital in Somerset and it was here that he died of a heart attack on 21st December 1950. He was sixty-three years old.

★★★

And what did become of Dan Billany? Was the mystery of his disappearance ever solved? The family think they know what happened. Roger Keyes gave them the clue when he referred them back to John Fleming's last view of Dan and David somewhere between Modena and Bologna. They looked back at the letter John had written in 1945 in response to the advertisement in The Daily Telegraph. It was all there, but at the time they had been reluctant to accept it. This is the story starting with John's words.

> After the Armistice of Sept 9th you may know we were released from the Camp 49 we were in, after which followed a period of hiding up. During the first 3 weeks of this I was with Alec and saw much of Dan who was with David nearby. We met daily and all of us were in good form ...

Early in October, the four of them had decided to head south. By this time, the heatwave was over and autumn had brought frequent rain and ever shortening days. They made good progress for the first couple of days and were relieved to find hospitable families who shared their food with them; generally it was macaroni soup or polenta, but it was hot and there was plenty of it. It was great to be able to go to bed with a full stomach, wrapped up in blankets in the straw of a barn or hayloft. And better still was the feeling of being free and on the way home. All four were in good spirits, fit and strong and ready to face whatever might be ahead.

Following directions given them by their hosts, they made good progress along side-roads and lanes and managed to evade the attention of the German troops who seemed to be everywhere. By the third evening they had reached a small village a few miles south of Modena. They were greeted cheerfully by a friendly farmer's wife who showed them to a dry, comfortable barn at the back of the property. They spent a happy evening with the family who provided them with a good meal and plenty of local wine, and retired early to the hayloft above the barn.

Shortly after midnight they were awoken by the farmer's wife who urgently whispered that the Germans were in the house looking for them. Someone in the village must have given them away. There was a scramble to get their boots on and all four left as fast as they could, scattering into the orchard at the back of the property. A thick white mist lay low over everything. They regrouped in a copse behind the farm and crouched together in the mist, waiting and listening. All was stillness and silence. Not a light was showing and it seemed that they had successfully evaded their captors.

There was a whispered consultation. Where to go now? Well, not back to the farm, they all agreed. Hiding up in the woods seemed the most sensible option, and then an early start in the morning, to get clear of the area before daybreak. They would just have to abandon the kit they had left in the hayloft. This included Dan's notebook, by which he set great store. Was he already writing another book, the story of his escape this time? Anyway, whatever it contained was important and he insisted he must go back for it. They waited a little longer, but all was still. So Dan and John crept slowly back towards the farmhouse. Suddenly a shot rang out; there was a German sentry beside the barn entrance. Both men dived into a nearby ditch and lay silent, half submerged, their faces pressed against the damp earth. They could hear footsteps and voices close by and catch glimpses of flashlights in the orchard. David and Alec must have been aware of what was happening too. Minutes passed and the sounds and lights retreated. John looked over his shoulder but there was no sign of Dan. All he could assume was that he had made his way along the ditch and climbed out at some further point. John took his chance. He cautiously stood up, pulled himself out of the ditch and with head down ran for the clump of trees where he had left the other two. There was no sign of either of them, but he couldn't wait and kept going until he was well away from the farm and safely concealed for the night.

John Fleming continued his journey alone and stayed at liberty for several more weeks, before being recaptured and transported to Germany. Dan, David and Alec were never seen again. Eventually their families came to accept that they must have died some time in October, and most probably in that ditch at the bottom of the orchard. One is reminded of a similar plight Dan invented for his hero Robbie Duncan in *The Opera House Murders*, only of course Robbie gets away.

I jumped like a rabbit for the ditch. I made it in three lightning hops, and slopped into it head first. As I swept the curtain of green scum from my face with my sleeve, the car screamed past, leaping like a horse on the uneven grass. It takes time to stop a big car going at that speed, and while they were braking, I was going along that ditch like the biggest and fastest water-rat that ever ran. You see, I happened to know that fifty yards along the ditch was a drainpipe, two feet in diameter, let into our garden wall, which carried the rains from the garden.

I cast a swift glance over my shoulder, through the long grasses which grew beside the ditch, and saw, quite a long way behind me, two men running hell for leather, along the road, each carrying a gun. They were making for the place where I had landed in the ditch. I jerked forward with the most earnest resolution, and went onward like a Christian; up to the thighs in mud, water, and slime. Ten feet ahead of me I saw the green, smelly mouth of the drainpipe, and it looked like the gate of Heaven to me. Ovid in his exile never yearned for the palaces of Rome as I yearned for the drainpipe. I made it with a last spasmodic flounder, and slithered in. It was seven feet long; it fitted me like a glove; and at the farther end of it was something that froze my heart inside me.

An iron grating went across the end. I was in my coffin.

Postscript

The story, in fact, did not finish there. Subsequent research by Roger Absalom at the National Archives in Washington has revealed that Dan Billany, David Dowie and Alec Harding journeyed much further than had originally been thought.

It was the practice for ex-prisoners on the run to leave with their Italian hosts a chit, simply a piece of paper bearing their thanks for the hospitality they had received, dated and signed with full name and address. The hope was that after the war, the British Government would compensate the Italian families who had risked so much to help the escapees. Sadly, any compensation paid was minimal and most received no more than a highly decorated certificate.

The chits were collected and are now stored in Washington, where Roger Absalom's investigations revealed that Dan, David and Alec not only left chits at Busseto, Soragna and Modena - this was where John Fleming lost sight of them - but considerably further south as well. The trail leads through Sasso Marconi, S. Benedetto Val di Sambro, Tornimparte and Capistrello. The last of these chits, dated 20th November 1943, was signed by all three.

It seems likely that they died of exposure somewhere in the Apennines shortly after this time, within a few days' march of the Allied lines.

Italy - the Winter of 1943-44

AUSTRIA

SWITZERLAND

YUGOSLAVIA

Soragna

Rezzanello
Camp 17

Fontanellato
Camp 49

Modena

FRANCE

• Sasso Marconi

• San Benedetto

Northern limit of
Allies' advance

Corsica

Tornimparte

• Capistrello

Rome

Capua
Camp 66

Sardinia

Naples

Sicily

BIBLIOGRAPHY

Absalom, Roger	A Strange Alliance, "Aspects of Escape and Survival in Italy 1943-1945". (Leo S Olschki Editore. Firenze. 1991)
Bell, Ian	...And Strength was Given (Tyndale & Panda 1989)
Billany, Dan	The Opera House Murders (Faber & Faber 1940)
Billany, Dan	The Magic Door (Thomas Nelson & Sons 1943)
Billany, Dan	The Cage (Longmans Green & Co 1949)
Billany, Dan	The Trap (Faber & Faber 1950)
Brown, R	The Waterfront Organisation in Hull 1870-1900 (The University of Hull 1972)
Campbell, John	Nye Bevan and the Mirage of British Socialism (Weidenfeld & Nicolson 1987)
Davies, Tony	When the Moon Rises (Leo Cooper 1973)
Davies, A J	To Build a New Jerusalem (Michael Joseph 1992)
Derry, Major Sam	The Rome Escape Line (Harrap 1960)
English, Ian (ed.)	Home by Christmas? (The Monte San Martino Trust 1997)
Foot, M.R.D & Langley, J.M.	M19, Escape and Evasion (Bodley Head 1979)
Geraghty, T	"A North-East Coast Town" (A Brown & Sons 1951)
Gilbert, Michael	Death in Captivity (Hodder & Stoughton 1952)
Gill, Alec	Hessle Road (Hutton Press 1987)
Hood, Stuart	Pebbles from my Skull (Hutchinson 1963)
Jordan, Martin	For You the War is Over (Peter Davies 1946)
Munton, Alan	English Fiction of the Second World War (Faber & Faber 1989)
Neill, A S	Summerhill (Victor Gollancz 1962)
Neillands, Robin	The Desert Rats (Weidenfeld & Nicolson 1991)
Newby, Eric	Love and War in the Apennines (Hodder & Stoughton 1971)
Nightingale, P R	The History of the East Yorkshire Regiment (Duke of Yorks Own) in the War of 1939 - 45 (W Sessions 1952)
Pelling, H & Reid, A J	A Short History of the Labour Party (Macmillan 1965)
Pitt, Barrie	The Crucible of War: Auchinleck's Command (Jonathan Cape 1980)
Smith, Peter	Massacre at Tobruk (William Kimber 1987)
Thompson, Michael	Hull Docklands (Hutton Press 1990)
Thorpe, Andrew	Britain in the 1930s (Blackwell 1992)
Whiting, Charles	The Long March on Rome, The Forgotten War (Century, 1987)
Woods, Rex	One Man's Desert - The Story of Captain Philip Gardner VC, MC (William Kimber 1986)
Worpole, Ken	Dockers and Detectives (Verve 1983)

INDEX